T0069780

PURE PRODUCTS OF AMERICA, INC.

Johns Hopkins: Poetry and Fiction
John T. Irwin, General Editor

A Narrative Poem by JOHN BRICUTH

Johns Hopkins University Press   *Baltimore*

This book has been brought to publication with the generous assistance of the Albert Dowling Trust and the Writing Seminars Publication Fund.

Johns Hopkins University Press
2715 North Charles Street
Baltimore, Maryland 21218-4363
www.press.jhu.edu

Library of Congress Cataloging-in-Publication Data

Bricuth, John, 1940–
    Pure Products of America, Inc.: a narrative poem / John Bricuth.
    pages cm
    ISBN 978-1-4214-1807-0 (pbk.: acid-free paper)—ISBN 978-1-4214-1808-7 (electronic)—ISBN 1-4214-1807-X (pbk.: acid-free paper)—ISBN 1-4214-1808-8 (electronic)
    I. Title.
    PS3552.R454P87 2015
    811'.54 dc23   2015004320

A catalog record for this book is available from the British Library.

Sections of this poem have appeared in *Boulevard.* The author thanks the editor of the magazine for permission to reprint those portions here.

Special discounts are available for bulk purchases of this book. For more information, please contact Special Sales at 410-516-6936 or specialsales@press.jhu.edu.

Johns Hopkins University Press uses environmentally friendly book materials, including recycled text paper that is composed of at least 30 percent post-consumer waste, whenever possible.

For my beloved Meme
For the outrageous Harold
For John and Jo Ann
And for Pat and Judy

CONTENTS

ACT ONE   Scene One   1

               Scene Two   31

               Scene Three   61

ACT TWO   Scene One   79

               Scene Two   107

               Scene Three   123

PURE PRODUCTS OF AMERICA, INC.

Act One

SCENE ONE

(A radio studio at a country music station in Texas.)

CHARLIE: Hey there! all you country music fans,
Ten-four, come back! Charlie Printwhistle here,
Comin' atcha in the P.M. on the

AM all the way from W-A-K-O,
Waco, Texas, grand ol' Babtist
Buckle on the Bible belt. That record you

Just heard's Clint Green's latest tune's
Been climbin' up the charts, "My Love's Not Some
Old Chew, My Heart's Not Your Spittoon," 'n' ain't

That sad but true? You know, I knew an orn'ry
Gal like that once, name of Alice Ann,
Alice Ann MacFutter's what she called

Herself (most likely wanted, church folks thought,
In sev'ral states), a Slurshee, same's that gal in
Olden days treated men like hogs

'Course, all the cowboys thought Miss Alice Ann
Was quite a looker, yessir, more they'd chase her,
Why, the worse she'd do 'em—not me though,

Always 'peared to me as how, caught out
In bright sunlight, both her eyes'd start
To cross, but that was in another town

(I think El Paso maybe), 'sides the gal is
Dead now anyhow, seems one night
The boys got liquored up, got fed up how

She'd fooled 'em, got so het up they jest up
'N' lynched her—strung her up ta the willow 'cross
The way, like in the song. But, folks, enough

High talk of you 'n' me 'n' mostly me,
'Cause Charlie's got a treat in store for all
You good God-fearin', fine hard-workin', plain

Tax-payin' people out in country music
Land, plus all you sad folks, shut-ins, 'n' such,
Seein' it's that time a week, time a day

Ol' Charlie has a guest stop by,
So's you can call right up 'n' hear yourself
A-talkin' on the air. That number here is

254-657-7468—
Try dialin' 254-Ol' Print.
Now, folks, my guest today's a man needs no

Introduction. Each time he comes to Waco
Preachin' his revival, why, he always
Stops in here 'n' says hello, 'n' no one

Out there list'nin' now don't know this fella's
Story: young man out a northeast Alabama,
Poor as dirt, works his way

Through high school, only recreation's when he's
Tryin' out ta make the wrestlin'
Team his freshman year, gets so good

He wins his weight division in the state
By graduatin' time, 'n' then turns pro,
Takes the name Big Bubba, wrestles as

The "good guy" in his matches, starts ta get a
Followin' 'n' fame, hits the big time,
Gets the big head, spendin' money right 'n'

Left, palin' 'round with this low
Entourage of hangers out 'n' hangers on,
Feet skiddin' on the slipp'ry slope: black drink 'n'

Bad women, foul bars 'n' fast cars,
'N' sure enough, he takes ta racin' stock cars
As a hobby, has so much success

Pretty soon he's drivin' as a pro.
'N' 'fore ya know it, here he comes a-wrestlin'
'N' a-racin' 'n' a-racin' 'n'

A-wrestlin' all across the South. Then one day—
Dirt track near Damascus, Georgia—rascal's
Drivin' in a race where he's been drinkin',

Matter a fac', boy's drunk as a furry owl,
Slam-bang! this great big pile-up at the turn,
Seven cars all mashed together, smokin' 'n'

A-sparkin', leakin' gas, they pull
Big Bubba out an instant jest before it all
Goes up, 'pears pert near dead, stuck in a

Coma three whole days 'n' nights 'n' when he
Wakens he's a different man, tells his ol'
Dusty-butt buddies fare thee well,

'Cause when that crack-up happened, why,
His soul went flying out his mouth (thing looked jest
Like a butterfly, he said), that's when a

Huge ol' hand ('bout size uva catcher's mitt)
Come swoopin' out the sky, 'n' what do you
Suppose? That butterfly jest nestles in

Its palm, 'n' sure enough, next instant Bubba's
Soul gets snatched up quick, right to that third-most
Heaven, where he hears dark, secret things man's

Tongue may not unfold (leastways, that's what
He told reporters gathered 'round his bed
When he come to), 'n' from that moment on

The Bubba that'd been was gone. (Can I
Get an Amen here?) Henceforth this boy's
A servant a the Lord, a-preachin', 'n'

A-teachin', 'n' a-healin' up the sick,
But when he comes ta town with his revival,
Well, there's some a where he come from still

Hangs on, 'cause all you folks ain't seen Big Bubba's
Service, why, he makes out like it's one
Big wrestlin' match, best two falls out a three,

Him against the Devil. First fall Bubba
Pins ol' Nick right quick. But then the second fall
Ol' Devil trips up Bubba, gets him in a

Hammerlock that lets him know
He ain't so strong or smart as what he thought.
Now comes the third fall, Devil's got him down,

Big Bubba's sweatin', usin' all his strength
Ta keep his shoulders off the mat—that's when
He casts his eyes above 'n' says, "Don't turn

Your face from this poor earthen vessel, Lord,
But help him in his need, so's he can leap 'n'
Glorify your name." 'N' quick like that!

Big Bubba feels his strength flow back, swings
His leg up over Satan's head, gets it
In a scissor hold, then flips him to

The mat 'n' squeezes tight till that dark angel
Ends up sayin' *uncle* ta the Lord.
Then later, as the dusky demon's walkin' off,

His second—that there evil dwarf (name of
Weaselsnot)—spreads the ropes ta let him
Pass, meanwhile a-brushin' off the boss's

Cape, 'n' Satan, kinda sidewise 'cross
His shoulder, says, "Thought sure I had ya that time,
Bubba, yes, I did. But when you call on

That Big Bully always comes 'n' pulls
Your bacon from the fire, well, I just says
Ta Weasel here, 'This ain't no fair fight no how, seems.'"

So Satan leaves, his tail between
His hooves. 'N', folks, now here's the man hisself,
The Rev'rend Ray Bob Elray, known to all his

Fans as plain Big Bubba. Bubba, always
Good to have you back at W-A-K-O.

BUBBA: Charlie, always good ta be here.

CHARLIE: You're here in Waco preachin' your revival
Out at Southern Babtist College, right?

BUBBA: Yeah, my special campus tour's a circuit

Runs through all the Texas schools, started
Off in Dallas, firin' up them high-toned
Methodists at SMU, then out ta

Fort Worth (Disciple a Christers there
At TCU), then onward to them Christian soldiers
Down at A&M, those party girls

'N' tea-sips at UT, I even brought
The gospel word to all them godless
Atheists at Rice, preached it three nights runnin'.

CHARLIE: I heard them Rice boys tried ta egg ya, Bubba.

BUBBA: Nawsir, they just tried ta egg me on,
Shoutin' catcalls when I'd preach, makin'

These here fartin' noises with their lips
Soon's I'd start ta speak in tongues. They even
Run a ringer on me (in amongst

The folks come up onstage there for the layin' on
A hands, the healin', dontcha know?),
This here fella's standin' there in line,

Humpback fella, lookin' like he's lame,
Pert near blind, 'n' when it comes his turn,
Wellsir, I beg Jehovah's help in tongues:

"A-willa-walla-willy-wooly-wooly"
(That starts the fartin' noises 'splodin' from
Balcony sure 'nough), then soon as they

Quiet down, I lay my hands on that poor sinner's
Forehead, sayin' loud, "Be gone, thou unclean
Spirit!," givin' his whole head a mighty

Shove ta show the Lord done cast the demon out.
Well, this here humpback rolls his eyes up,
Faintin' dead away, fallin' backwards

'Fore he's caught by waitin' deacons like
They do 'n' laid out on the floor when all at
Once the humpback starts ta pee hisself,

'N' lord! this pilgrim's bladder's pumpin' like a
Gusher, more 'n any man, more 'n any
Horse, way more 'n any elly-

Phant can hold! This big ol' yella puddle
Out his trouser leg starts crawlin' 'cross
The floor till all the other folks

On stage're standin' kinda tippy-toe,
Lookin' funny, mebbe like they'd like ta
Cut 'n' run. A course the Rice boys in the

Balcony're howlin' like coyotes.
(Come ta find out later, this here fella
Weren't no humpback after all, jest some

Heathen been relievin' uv hisself,
Fer more 'n ten days runnin', in a big ol'
Rubber bladder, then afore he come on

Stage there fer the healin', why, he straps
This bag a pee across his back inside his
Coat 'n' runs a tube right down his trouser leg.

He's plugged the end with wax so's when
He falls flat on his back, the plug goes pop!
'N' he cuts loose.) Well now, I'm standin' there,

A-hearin' all the Rice boys yellin', "Preacher,
Play like ol' man Mose 'n' part the Yella
Sea," a-seein' that it's all a trick, but thinkin'

"Well, sir, I'll return 'em good
Fer evil," 'cause, accordin' ta the gospel,
That's the way ta heap up coals a fire

Right on their heads, so when I raise my hand
Fer silence, sayin' as I always do
When facin' heathen catcalls, "Like the Lord,

I'll turn the other cheek," why, just like that!,
As if they'd all rehearsed it, these here wolfsheads
In the balcony turn 'round, drop trou,

'N' moon the Lord's own servant in His temple.
(That's when the fartin' noises start a-burstin'
Just like bombs.) Wellsir, right away

A bugle sounds from somewhere up above
A-signalin' this fella on the floor,
His eyes pop open, up he jumps (by now

This dog's done emptied out the pee sack on
His back), he starts in shoutin', "Look, I'm cured,
I'm saved, Big Bubba took my hump away!"

Then these here other infidels start chantin' loud as
Thunder, "Bubba took his hump away,
Big Bubba took his hump away!"

Sure 'nough, right quick come two more bugle notes
'N' all the chantin' stops like on a dime,
Then one more note 'n' half the balcony

Begins, "Big Bubba took his hump away!" till that
Sets off the other half a-shoutin',
"Bubba, give it back, Bad Bubba, give it

Back!" 'n', Print, it's back 'n' forth like that
Till Bubba just can't stand no more abuse.
That's when he calls upon Jehovah, Lord a

Hosts, ta smite the vile Amalekite,
Ta burn his barn 'n' blight his corn, then break
His reed 'n' blast his seed as once he done

In days of yore. But that was then 'n' this is
Now, 'n' Bubba's back here, Print, in four-square
Gospel country testifyin' ta your list'ners

What indignities the Lord's own
Servant suffers preachin' to the heathen—
But that's ta say, His grace is great enough.

CHARLIE: More stars there in your crown, Big Bubba—that's
              What I predict. But how 'bout takin' calls 'n' talkin'
              Some. Switchboard's all lit up.

BUBBA: Proud to, put 'em on 'n' let 'er rip.
CHARLIE: Caller One, you're on the air, go 'head.
CALLER ONE: Hello?
CHARLIE: Yes, Caller One, you're on the air.

CALLER ONE: That you, Charlie?

CHARLIE: Yes it is, I'm here with
Bubba. Whatcha wanna ask him, darlin'?

CALLER ONE: Preacher, tell me somethin'.

BUBBA: Surely, try to...

CALLER ONE: When the Lord lets bad things happen sometimes,
When He lets a woman ain't had nothin'
In her life but trouble have one thing

So sweet it more 'n makes up fer the rest—
A precious child, ya know, a boy that grows up
Straight 'n' strong, 'spite the fact his pa

Run off when he was only five, 'n' then,
With years, the Lord a-keepin' watch, the boy
Becomes a young man with an open, trusting

Heart 'n' decent ways, 'cause that's the way
His mother raised him, brought him up ta love his
Country too, 'cause, Bubba, after 9/11

Nothin' else'd do but out a
High school, why, he had ta join the service.
Army sent him to Iraq a year ago,

'N', preacher, six months back come Monday
Was the day my boy got killed, got blown up
By a roadside bomb, 'n', Bubba, what I

Want ta know is why the Lord God let
My Tommy die like that. That boy was all
I had, 'n' all I'm ever gonna have, 'n', Bubba,

How I loved him. I get so lonesome
When I think about the way he looked,
The way he made me laugh, oh God, I jest...

BUBBA: Now, sister, please, ya gotta stop that cryin'.
Ya know, that question "why" is one I've never
Known the Lord ta answer all the years

I've been out preachin'. Seems the best that any
Man can do's jes' make a guess 'n' trust
The Lord's own wisdom. Still, I'll tell ya what I

Think. Ya know, the Lord when He creates
A soul, why, He jest gives each one a little
Diff'rent turn, some a 'em are smarter,

Some a 'em are kinder, some He gives
An extra big capacity fer lovin'.
Well, ya see, when He does that, He's got

Ta send that person someone special they can
Love, so's they can use that big capacity
He gave 'em. Well now, I'd say that's what

He done with you 'n' your boy Tommy, was it?
CALLER ONE: Yes, it's Tommy, preacher.
BUBBA: See, but sometimes
When a person who can love so much

Gives their whole heart ta one who's extra special,
Well, it's like the Bible says, The Lord
Our God's a jealous God. He's made us so's

We'd love Him most of all, ya see, 'n' don't
Take kindly when some creature that He give
The gift a life to goes ta placin' someone else

Above Him in their hearts. So what's
He do sometimes but catch that extra-special
Person there right gently by the wrist

'N' lead him home, that way a-bringin' back
The heart that loved him, dontcha see?, ta where
Its treasure's truly stored, where rust can't ever

Reach, as Matthew says, or any moth
Corrupt, 'n', sister, if you'll only keep on
Trustin' in the Lord, then when He gathers

You into His bosom, why, that boy a
Yours'll be there waitin' with a hug.

CALLER ONE: Yes, Bubba, but I get so lonesome sometimes,

'Swhat I'm sayin'. Dinner time 'n' after's
'Bout the worst. I miss the way we used ta
Sit there at the table, how he'd tell me

'Bout his day or plan the future, him
Daydreamin' right out loud, sayin' when
He won the lotto how he'd build his ma

The house she'd dreamed uv. Well, ya know, that's all
Gone now 'n', preacher, seems here lately when I
Go ta climb the stairs at night there's such

A load a lonesome sorrow weighin' on my
Shoulders ev'ry step keeps gettin' higher
Till it seems like times I jest won't make it.

BUBBA: Sister, dontcha know, there's someone else
Had this ol' weary load ta carry so's he'd
Stumble on the cobblestones 'n' fall?

That's why them Romans found a man named Simon
Helped Him with the weight, 'n', sister, dontcha
Think that Man a Sorrows don't know what you've

Been a-feelin' uv an evenin' on
Them stairs? Why shoot! 'course He does, 'n' jest like
Simon helped Him tote his load, the Lord'll

Help you bearin' yours. He's there beside you
On them steps at night, jest reach out till you
Find Him, hear? 'n' somethin' you just said

Come ringin' like the Lord give Bubba here
A sign in your own words a what he's 'sposed ta
Tell ya. See, that boy of yours'd planned

Ta build his ma a house she'd always dreamed uv
When he could. Well, dontcha know the Lord
Prepares a special place ta welcome ev'ry

Soul that comes ta glory, maybe it's
A favorite spot or time a year, like if
A person loved the winter time, then it's

A cozy room beside a fire, or maybe
If that person liked the spring, then He'd
Jest fix 'em up a garden, see? 'n' since

Your boy is there now with the Lord, why, he can
Tell Him 'bout the place you'd always dreamed uv.
Now whatcha think that boy a yours'ud say?

CALLER ONE: Oh, Bubba, Tommy knows I love a garden
               Best of all. I'd always tell him 'bout
               The one my parents had in Nacogdoches

When I weren't no bigger 'n a minute.
Growin' up, how I loved that spot.

BUBBA: Sure you did! 'n' that's jest what he'd tell

The Lord, 'n' then come mornin' both a them'ud
Head outdoors, all set ta fix your special
Place, the Lord'ud take a shovel 'n' a

Hoe, 'n' Tommy'd take a waterin' can
'N' lots a plants 'n' seeds, 'n' they'd commence
Ta put some roses 'n' begonias in

CALLER ONE: No, sir, Bubba, Tommy knows my fav'rites're
Pink peonies all shaggy-headed
Like a lion's mane—'n' lilacs too, 'n' blue

Hydrangea flowers 'bout the size a soft balls.
BUBBA: Sure! 'n' see, he'd tell the Lord that so's they'd
Have that garden ready when you came,

'Cause when you're born again ta brightness, bustin'
Out the dark grave's tunnel, well now, howdy!,
What's the first thing meets your eye but it's

Your parents' garden waitin', with your boy there
At the gate, your ma 'n' pa up close
Behind him, with the Lord in back a them,

All gettin' set ta give your neck a hug.
CALLER ONE: Oh, Bubba, do you think that's what'll happen?
BUBBA: Sister, I believe it 'cause the Bible

Tells me so. You'll see that boy again.
CALLER ONE: Oh, preacher, then, God bless ya! Oh, God bless ya!
BUBBA: Sister, God bless *you*! 'n' trust in Him.

CHARLIE: Well, folks, what say we give ol' Bubba here
            A break 'n' play some country music. How
            About it, Bubba? Will ya hang around here

            Fer another segment?
BUBBA: Proud to, Charlie.
CHARLIE: Well, folks, Bubba'll be back soon, but now
            Ol' Charlie's got a golden oldie for ya,

            T. Texas Tubb 'n' the Troubadours singin'
            "Clyde, Clyde, I Do Believe, the Dog's Got
            My Shoes"...We're off the air now, Ace.

            Boy, howdy!, that ol' line a yours keeps gettin'
            Smoother ev'ry time you come to town, but what
            I never know, not even after

            All the times you've been here's, whether you
            Believe that stuff, or you're just mighty good
            At makin' like you do. I must admit, Ace,

            When you had 'em all there in the garden
            At the end, ol' Charlie's eyes began ta
            Puddle up.
BUBBA: Hellfire, Charlie, ev'rybody

            Knows you cry at card tricks, that's
            No test. 'Sides whether I believe or not's a
            Matter don't concern, from my side, no one

            But the Lord 'n' me, while them folks needs
            The comfortin', why, it don't make no diff'rence
            Whether I believe or I'm just good at

Makin' like I do, 'cause either way
For them the comfortin' comes through.

CHARLIE: Well, Ace,
That's answer's pert near slick as what you told

That grievin' mother 'bout her son just now
Was smooth.

BUBBA: Say, whatcha think here, Charlie, I'm
Some kinda actor playin' like the Lord's

True servant? Seems ta me if I'd a mind ta,
I could turn them words around, 'cause *you're* not
Just the kinda person you pretend ta

Be here, neither. Whatcha think your fans,
Ya know, that club a yours, the Waco Wackos,
The Waco Wankers.

CHARLIE: The Waco Wahoos.

BUBBA: Yeah, that's

The one, whatcha think they'd say if they's
Ta hear how you was only foolin' bein'
Home folks, huh?

CHARLIE: Howzat, Ace?

BUBBA: Why, shoot!,

On air there, Print, I swear, your mouth's so fulla
Grits 'n' gravy even I can't understand ya times,
Yet seems as how I recollect now

Someone told me once, back in your
Early days, you went ta Yale 'n' graduated
Some Come Louder, while ol' Bubba here

Jes' barely made it through an Alabama
High school, but he knowed that gal
In olden times that turned men into hogs

Weren't named no Slurshee, neither.

CHARLIE: Well, ya caught
Me, Ace. That's why we get along so well,
We each appreciate the "nuanced savoir

Faire" (that's how they'd yawp it up at Yale),
"The subtle subtext grounds the other character's
Performance"—seein' we're both troupers

In the business they call "show." But since
We're talkin' business, what's the lowdown 'bout
This rumor has you startin' your own comp'ny.

BUBBA: Yes, sir. Had to, Print, the ministry's
Done gotten such a followin' here of late,
'N' folks keep sendin' Bubba cards 'n' letters

Askin' can he recommend 'em things that's pure,
'Cause now'days, well, sir, most things aint 'n'
Most God-fearin' folks can't find the stuff

That is (there's so much fornicatin' with
Fornography, adultery from products
That's adulterated), why, I just figured

When it comes ta findin' pure things, Print, I
Wouldn't recommend 'em only, I'd
Provide 'em, so I called my firm "Pure Products

Of America, Incorporated,"
Started out with bibles, went ta hymn books,
Then I had the choir, ya know the one

Accomp'nies Bubba at revivals, make a
Two CD collection titled *Bubba's*
Fifty Favorite Hymns, durn thing sold so

Well we just brought out a four CD-er,
Bubba's Hunnert Favorite Hymns. Our next move
Took us into cakes 'n' candies, pure ones, see?,

Divinity 'n' angel food,
Not your devil's food or fudge. Seems lately
Here demand has got so great for Bubba's

Products, why, he's had ta start franchisin'
His endorsements. That's the kinda lingo
All them Wall Street fellas like ta sling,

But, Print, it works like this: 'spose there's somethin'—
Say it's jams 'n' jellies—Bubba's gettin'
Lotsa cards 'n' letters 'bout, inquirin'

What's the purest one ta buy, 'n' maybe
Bubba dudn't feel like startin' up a
Business buyin' fruit, 'n' cookin' it,

'N' puttin' up preserves, so what's he do?
He goes ta three, four comp'nies makin' jams
'N' cuts a deal, says, "Look here, boys, two ways

That we can do this, either you sell me your
Stuff in jars without no labels"—which case
I can slap one on 'em sayin' "Bubba's

Best Preserves" 'n' sell 'em through the mail
Direct ta all the faithful, see?—"or you can
Pay a fee 'n' I'll endorse your whole durn

Line a jams 'n' jellies with a statement
You can put right on the jar: 'Bubba
Guarantees this stuff is PURE,' with my own

Picture there beside it 'n', beneath,
My signature."

CHARLIE: Yeah, but Bubba, tell me,
How do you decide which one's the purest?

D'ya have a chemist analyze 'em?

BUBBA: Nawsir,
Way I do it's patterned after that ol'
Houston lawyer Percy Foreman when he

Got a woman off scot-free at trial
For murderin' the millionaire she'd married
Just six months before. Seems after court let out

This high society matron braces
Percy, says, "Now, lawyer, aintcha 'shamed,
Lettin' brazen killers loose? The Lone Star

State was dustin' off the Huntsville hot squat
For her, till you put your big oar in."
Well, Percy he just smiles, eye takes on this

Glint, he tilts his Stetson back some, drawls,
"Why, darlin', dontcha know, my fee's her punishment?"

CHARLIE: Hell, Bubba, what's 'at got ta do with findin'

Jams that's pure?

BUBBA: Why, Charlie, dontcha see?
Ol' Percy's fee's sa big no one 'ud ever hire him
'Less'n they was in a pure D jam, guilty as sin

'N' needin' A-1 lawyerin' ta save their
Skin 'n', see, that's just the way it is
With comp'nies think their stuff is pure 'n' pay

My fee ('n' just 'tween you 'n' me, Print, it's
A whopper). Ain't no comp'ny fool enough ta
Run the risk of losin' all that money

If they knew their stuff weren't pure, not ta
Mention, rousin' up the wrath a Bubba
'N' the Lord, who don't take kindly ta no

Comp'ny foolin' His true servant—un'erstan,
Print, what I'm sayin'?

CHARLIE: Print could say he
He did, but he'd be lyin', 'n' Print don't want no

Trouble with the Lord, God knows, but since you
Brought the subject up of fees 'n' since
We both been talkin' 'bout ourselves in what

They call "third-person present prétence," didn't
Bubba bring his ol' pal Print a present
Here today?

BUBBA: You're right, I plumb forgot.

There ya are.

*(Bubba takes an envelope out of his inside coat pocket
and hands it to Charlie. Charlie weighs it for a moment
in his hand, then looks inside.)*

CHARLIE: Seems ta me the pot's
A little light, lot less 'n what it was
The last time you was through.

BUBBA: Why, Charlie, that's

The first installment. See, I got this business
Man'ger owlhoot once I started up the
Comp'ny (fella used ta work for Enron,

Reg'lar hotshot), well now, seems this fella
Noticed when Big Bubba'd show up on a
Talk show somewhere, drummin' up some int'rest,

Spreadin' word he's back in town a-preachin'
His revival, well, this fella noticed
When we'd bring the talk-show host a little

Somethin', just our way a sayin' thanks
For havin' Bubba on, why, some a these here
DJs, soon as Bubba'd leave the show, 'ud never

Mention him again or his
Revival 'spite the fact we'd be in town
Another three nights or a week, so what this

Fella says is why not make the DJ's
Thank-you gift a little somethin' down, just on
Account, then tell him we'll be list'nin' in each

Day, countin' up the times he
Mentions Bubba's preachin' there in town,
'N' that way if he keeps it up so lotsa

Folks turn out, why, then, time comes ta
Leave, the DJ gets another little
Gift, say, maybe two percent of what's

Collected from the faithful ev'ry night Big
Bubba preaches they pass the basket after.
Sometimes there's a DJ don't trust

Bubba on the numbers, so we tell him
Come on down yourself 'n' count the house,
Then watch the deacons total up the take

From all the baskets. That us'ally shuts 'em up.
CHARLIE: You really pack 'em in there, dontcha, Bubba?
BUBBA: Bubba's tent is big, ev'ry race 'n'

Creed 'n' color's welcome, "red 'n' yellow,
Black 'n' white, they are precious in His
Sight."
CHARLIE: Yeah but, look here, that don't mean

You don't turn 'em into green, 'cause Bubba
Loves the little children uv the world.
BUBBA: Charlie, you're a heathen piece a work.

CHARLIE: Tell me 'bout that two percent, what's it
Out of, gross or net?
BUBBA: Why, net, a course.
It takes a heap a mammon just ta do

The Lord's own work, 'n' whatcha take me for?
CHARLIE: Well, once I took ya for a redneck holy
Roller, Ace, but lately here you're shapin' up

Ta be the Donald Trump a holy
Rollers. Aintcha 'fraid now, Bubba, one a
These here days some DJ with his nose

Bent outa joint might jest blow the whistle
On ya, tell the papers 'bout these little
Gifts.
BUBBA: Why, Charlie, one already did.

This fella out in Muleshoe had a cousin
Up in New York workin' at the *Times*,
Jest some smarty pants spends his day

A-writin' stories pokin' fun at "hypocrites
'N' other right-wing preachers," 'swhat he
Says. Well, this here fella shows up, nosin'

'Round, askin' questions, actin' like he's
"Down home" folks. Why, shoot!, I see'd right through him
In a second, wouldn't talk ta him

At all, same for all my people once I
Told 'em what he was. Say, listen, Print,
They wouldn'ta pissed in that boy's mouth if all

His teeth'd been on fire. So then this fella
Turns up at revivals, sittin' in
The crowd, makin' like he's got the Lord's

Good News when all he's got's this tape recorder
In his pocket seein' can he get folks sayin'
Somethin' he can twist, 'n' turn ta fun.

Wellsir, I'd had enough, so this one night
(We were in San Saba, as I recollect)
Come the middle of the sermon,

I jest stop 'n' point him out a-sittin'
Sly-like in the second row. I says,
"Ya know, folks, Bubba's given Satan sucha

Drubbin' here of late, the Devil's sent a
Special tempter in our midst, this blue-state,
Yella-dog newsman sneakin' round, dead set on

Trippin' up the Lord's true servant." Wellsir,
All the brethren started lookin' hard-eyed
At this fella, clinchin' up their fists,

Tightenin' their jaws, but this here yayhoo's
Smart, ya see, he wouldn't make eye contact,
Knowin', soon's he did, why, he'd be in

Fist city quick, so he jest sits there lookin'
At his lap, meek as milk, till this
Ol' Texas gal who's sittin' right behind him

Rises up 'n' says real loud, "Seems
Ta me if these here men can't run a varmint
Out a God's own temple, why, us women

Got ta take a hand," 'n' with them words
This gal rares back 'n' shouts, "Be gone, you Satan!"
Then she hawks a grey-green oyster up from

Way back in her throat 'n' spits it right on
Top a that boy's head. Next thing ya know,
All the women sittin' round him stand 'n'

Start ta spittin' on him too 'n' by
The time he makes it to the aisle this fella's
Pert near drenched. I swear, Print, you'da almost

Felt plumb sorry for this pilgrim if he
Hadn'ta been an agent a the devil,
But when he went ta dry his face he pulled

A red bandanna from his pocket, see,
That's when I said, "That's jest a part a his
Disguise as down-home folks," 'n' so I set

My face against him, Print, but lookee here,
That didn't make no diff'rence 'cause by then
He'd made the aisle 'n' got his face dried off when

This tall gal who musta been a good
Ten feet away takes aim 'n' arcs a big one
Like a mortar shell right smack dab on this

Fella's coat lapel, 'n' howdy! he starts
Runnin' up the aisle 'n' ain't been heard from since.
The idea a this yayhoo thinkin'

He'd play gotcha with the Lord's true servant!
Well, come Judgment Day, we'll see just who's got
Who. Why, I can see the headline in

The *Times* right now: "WHOLE WORLD ENDS—
MINORITIES 'n' WOMEN HARDEST HIT." But listen,
Print, it won't be them that takes the hit,

CHARLIE: But all them high-hat lib'ral journalists.
              The booth's givin' me the high sign, Bubba,
              Newsbreak's pert near done, get set, we're on

The air again in three...two...one...Hey there!
All you country music fans, we're here with
Rev'rend Ray Bob Elray, takin' calls,

So you good folks just call in here, y'hear?
The number's 254-Ol' Print. Well, now,
I only wish you church folks coulda heard

The words a comfort Bubba spoke ta Charlie
In the break. Why, at one point, I jest
Had ta holler, "Someone come 'n' get me!

'Cause I feel the Holy Spirit's true
Anointin'!" Caller Two, you're on the air
With Bubba. What's on your mind?

CALLER TWO:
                                                 Charlie, got a

Question on the Scriptures for the preacher.

BUBBA: Go 'head.

CALLER TWO: In *Genesis*, twenty-five 'n' twenty-
Six...

BUBBA: Yeah, that's the tale a Isaac's young 'uns,

Jacob, Esau, all you folks ain't got
Your bibles handy—

CALLER TWO: Well, now, preacher, seems
I recollect how even though this Esau

Was the elder, why, the Lord allows as
How the elder's got ta serve the younger,
Bow before his brother Jacob, then the

Lord lets Jacob swindle Esau, steal his
Birthright for a mess a potage, next He
Looks the other way while Jacob puts

A sheepskin on his back ta make like he's that
Hairy rascal Esau—all so's he can fool
His pa who's pert near blind 'n' get

The blessing Isaac meant ta give the elder.
Now then, preacher, what I want ta know is
Where's the justice there, why's the Lord

Let Jacob get away with this 'n' favor
Him above the elder?

BUBBA: Like I said ta
Caller One, that "why"'s a real stumper when

It comes ta knowin' what Jehovah's
Up to. Still, reason with me here a spell,
Let's see what we can figure. Now the

Lord a Hosts when He reveals hisself
Ta men takes on the image of a Pa,
This stern ol' Dad whose stiff decisions can't

Be questioned. Well, a first-born son believes
He has a birthright, but in Job it says,
"Compared to God, what man is justified?"

No son has got a right that he can claim
Against *that* Father, so ta illustrate that
Through the sons a Isaac, why, the Lord

Removes his favor from the elder 'n' bestows it
On young Jacob, showin' when it
Comes ta God's own will, "the wind blows where

It listeth." Then the Lord, ta caution Jacob
'Bout the way he fooled his pappy inta
Thinkin' he's his brother, why, He let

Ol' Jacob's sons that's jealous a their daddy's
Favorite, Joseph, trick their pa, tellin'
Him how Joseph done got et up by a

Beast, then showin' him Joe's coat a many
Colors dipped in lamb's blood, when they really
Sold the boy ta slavers down in Egypt.

But tell me, Caller Two, jest what's your
Stake in this? Why'zat Scripture passage
Come ta mind?

CALLER TWO: Well, preacher, seems ta me

That Bible story says a lot ta folks
Now'days, folks that think they're so durn smart,
Talkin' God, till times they think they *are* God,

Then let theirselves be fooled by young 'uns set ta
Turn their pa against the eldest son,
Ta steal his birthright, seize the patrimony,

Not ta mention all their pappy's money.
Preacher, whatcha think about a father'd
Let hisself be hoodwinked like ol' Isaac?

BUBBA: Well now, Caller Two, we've all got our own
Problems, I'm sure that yours'll work out somehow.
Listen, folks, Big Bubba's gotta run...

CHARLIE: Say what?
BUBBA: Just look at that ol' clock there
On the wall, the time done got away from
This here preacher, he's expected any

Moment out at Southern Babtist College
Gettin' preparations set ta kick his
Big revival off tonight at eight.

We're there at Brann Memorial Hall, so all
You folks a-list'nin' in, jest come on down.
'N' thank you, Charlie, havin' this ol' preacher

On so's he can jaw a spell with all
Your list'ners.
CHARLIE: Thank *you*, Bubba, comin' on here
Bringin' words a wisdom, words a grace.

Time now, folks, ta take a commercial break
We're off the air now, Ace. What gives? I thought
Ya said you'd stay another segment.

BUBBA: Yeah, but

All at once I recollected somethin'
I forgot.

CHARLIE: Ya know, that Caller Two there
Towards the end—who the voice sorta

Sounded like...

BUBBA: Nawsir, I don't think so.
Jest some nut—Big Bubba gets 'em all the time.
So tell me, gonna make it down

Tonight ta count the house? 'night's the night
We televise the opening hour, do it
Live there weekly fer that new Can't-Beat-

The-Bible Cable Network.

CHARLIE: Well, since ya told me
'Bout this sweet DJ arrangement, why,
A poor ol' sinner like myself jest can't

Afford ta miss them golden words.

BUBBA: Sounds good—
You know Slim, ol' colored gent's been with me
Since my wrestlin' days? I'll leave word so's

He'll bring ya back stage soon as you
Arrive.

CHARLIE: Sure do, me 'n' Slim're pals. See ya,
Bubba. Break a leg Hey, there, all you

Country music fans, it's Charlie Printwhistle
By his lonesome. Bubba's headed back
For his revival out at Southern Babtist

College 'long 'bout eight tonight. What say
We have some country music now? 'Fore Bubba
Left he said, "Now, Charlie, play a song

Mentions the good Lord's name," so here's that great
Ol' jug band tune from yesteryear, Uncle Fud's
Tone Rangers pickin' 'n' singin' "Never Ever

Fell In Love, But Lord's! Been Lotsa Times
I've Stepped In It." Pin ol' Satan ta the mat
'N', Bubba, don't let go or Charlie's done fer sure.

Act One

SCENE TWO

(Backstage as Slim Daniels and Charlie Printwhistle enter stage left.)

SLIM: Right this way, Mr. Charlie. Stand right
          Here so's you can peek out through the curtain,
          Watch them chu'ch folks comin' in 'n' count 'em

          Good.
CHARLIE: Thank ya kindly, Slim, but that
          Ain't what I come fer. Me 'n' Bubba's been buds
          Long enough ain't never had no call

          Ta doubt him on the numbers. Naw, I jes'
          Come by ta catch the show.
SLIM: 'N' it's a good'un too—
          We packs the hall plumb full.
CHARLIE: I know. But seems like

          I been pluggin' Bubba's preachin'
          On the air 'n' hadn't caught his act
          In two, three years, thought maybe Ace'd added

          Magic tricks or fireworks, what with this here
          Syndicated TV show 'n' all.
          'Dja hear yer boss a-jawin' on the radio

Today?

SLIM: Yessir, that's a job a work
My Bobby don't let no one do but Slim.
I listen in, then count the times the DJ

Mentions our revival after Bobby
Leaves the show.
CHARLIE: So tell me, how'd ol' Charlie
Do?
SLIM: Why, Mr. Print, you're jes' about

The best—every fifteen minutes jes' like
Clockwork till the end.
CHARLIE: 'Dja hear that second
Caller Bubba talked to? I'da swore

There at the end sounded like it might be
One or t'other a the twins.
SLIM: That's right,
Mr. Charlie. It was Nicky actin' mean.

CHARLIE: So what I heard's the truth?
SLIM: What's that?
CHARLIE: Talk is Nick 'n' Bubba had a fight
'N' Bubba threw him off the show, "removed

Him from the ministry" 'sway I heard it put.
SLIM: I swear I've never seen two boys
Look more alike than Nick 'n' Jesse, jes' ta

Be sa diff'rent down inside.
CHARLIE: Well, you should know,
You hepped ta raise 'em.
SLIM: Yessir. After
Becca died, I surely did. Hepped raise

Young Donna too.

CHARLIE: Speakin' a Donna, where's
She at?

SLIM: Why, Mr. Charlie, she was here
Jes' now rehearsin' with the choir, 'n' Lawd!

Can that gal sing. She always ends by doin'
"Jes' a Closer Walk with Thee." Seems Donna
Knows her Uncle Slim likes that one best.

Spec' she'll be back thisaways directly.

CHARLIE: Seems ta me you been with Bubba jest
About the longest stretch a anyone.

SLIM: Sure 'nough, been with him from the start,
Matter a fact, befo' the start. I worked
For Bobby's parents on the farm. When he left home

Ta be a wrestler after high school,
Bobby's Pa said, "Slim, you're older than
My boy by some, 'n' jes' a whisker wiser,

'Sides the fact you been his friend since he
'Uz crawlin' in the dirt, 'n' Ma 'n' me
Knows you're a Christian. What I want is you

Go with him whilst he's travelin', keep him off
From bad companions, see my boy stands upright
With the Lawd." That's what his pappy aksed me,

That's what Slim Daniels did. I stayed with him
Fo' forty years, through ups 'n' downs,
'N' thicks 'n' thins, 'n' come nigh quittin'

Only once—time he cussed me out 'n' called
Ol' Slim a loser.

CHARLIE: Naw! I don't believe it.
SLIM: Yessir! Yes, he did. Back in them racin'

Days, when he 'uz drinkin' liquor all the time
With them ol' white trash fellas from
The track. I told him what his Pappy'd say if he

Could see him, Mr. Print, that's when
He told me, "Get away, you raggedy-ass'd
Loser." The boy was drunk 'n' showin' off

Fer all them rednecks sittin' 'roun' there laughin'.
Wellsir, I walks right up 'n' says, "Young Bobby
Elray, ain't I knowed you since you wadn't

Big enough ta jump a punkin'? 'N' ain't I
Had your back fo' all these years?
Tell me when Slim Daniels ever let you down.

Go on, boy, jes' say when. Well now, I'd sure 'nough
Rather be a black man in this world
Than be the kinda man 'ud disrespect

His oldest, realest friend, jes' showin' off
Fo' some ol' white trash fellas couldn't give a
Damn about him." Said that—yes, I did,

Then turned my back 'n' walked away. Here come
Next mornin' there's a knockin' on the door
Up there where I 'uz stayin' at. 'N' Lawd, if it ain't

Bobby standin' there, 'most lookin' like
A drowndéd pup, them big ol' horse-turd tears
Up in his eyes, sayin' how Slim Daniels 'sbeen

Might' near the only body in this
World ever give a hoot about him
'Cept his Ma 'n' Pa, 'n' that I knew

That thing he said last night was jes' the liquor
Talkin', how he couldn't rightly say
Jes' what he'd do if I'se ta up 'n' quit him.

Well, I told him, "Seems ta me, when folks
Get liquored up, they says what they been thinkin'
Deep inside, things their manners wouldn't

Let 'em say out loud col' sober." But since
I give my word ta Bobby's Pa, that man that
Always treated Slim 'n' his whole fam'ly

Right, I tol' him how I wadn't 'bout ta
Quit him, Mr. Print, nawsir. But if
He kept that drinkin' up, there'd sure 'nough come a

Time he'd quit this world 'n' ev'ryone
That's in it. Then where'd his ol' pal Slim be then?
That's when he promised, raised his hand up high

Ta heaven swearin' how he'd never get that
Drunk again. Well now, that lasted jest about
Two weeks. The thing that stopped the drinkin's

When he had that crack-up near Damascus
'Bout a month right after. Had him laid up
In that clinic, dead as a beef pert near.

Stayed there with him that whole time when he
'Uz sleepin'. Nurses tried ta run me off.
I'd go, but I'd sneak back. Come night

I'd take aholt a Bobby's hand 'n' haul him back,
Say, "Bobby, where you gone? Get that
Soul a yours back down here in this bed.

Ya likes ta play at hide-'n'-seek—been like that
Since we both 'uz boys—but this here's
'Bout enough." Then when Bobby waked on up,

Middle a the night, what's the first thing
That boy sees but Slim there dozin' in a chair
Upside the bed, 'n' when he tol' me

Where he'd been 'n' what he'd heard, I knew
The reason why Slim Daniels first got put here
On this earth. The Lawd done raised Hisself

A prophet up, a teacher sent ta keep
His people in the way, then set Slim Daniels
Here befo', jes' ta be the boy's

Right arm. Well now, I done been that fo' almost
Forty years, been right there with him when he
Started his revivals, with him on the night he

First saw Becca walkin' in the tent—
'N' Mr. Print, if that gal weren't an angel
Uv the Lawd I never hopes ta see one—

There the day they both got hitched in chu'ch,
'N' there the night the twins got born, up ta
That big hospital in Memphis, there that

Other night when Bobby got the phone call
'Bout the crash, how Becca 'n' her sister,
Sister's husban' too, all done got killed.

CHARLIE: Yeah, Slim, I remember, 'long 'bout twenty
Years ago.

SLIM: Yessuh, eighteen years
This April. They 'uz drivin' back all night,

Aimed ta join the show come our next stop.
('Member Becca's sister played the organ
With the choir, 'n' Bill, the husban', sang

The solo parts, that's where young Donna gets
The music from, her Ma 'n' Pa). Bill's Gran'ma
Died the day befo' when we 'uz out in Alpine

Holdin' our revival. Soon's we'd finished, why,
Those three drove all the way ta Brownsville
Fo' the fun'ral, left the twins 'n' Donna

Back with me 'n' Bobby. Comin' back,
Brother Bill 'uz drivin', tried ta make it
In ta Amarilla over night

(That's the place the show was headed), pohlice
Figured how he musta fell ta sleep
Behint the wheel, hit that highway 'butment goin'

Eighty—out there on that road jes'
North a Plainview.

CHARLIE: I recollect the picture
In the paper, pert near crushed that big ol'

Buick.

SLIM: Yessuh, that sister sittin'
Passenger side, jes' took her head clean off,
'N' Becca sleepin' in the back, that sweet gal

Never saw the blow that hit her. Next few
Days I thought the Lawd 'n' me'd lost
Our Bobby sure. Why, the boy jes' walkin'

'Roun' like he 'uz poleaxed. I recollect
One evenin', after all the funeralin' got done,
We 'uz up ta Bobby's room in that

Hotel when Bobby fetches up a bottle full
A that ol' devil brew Jim Beam.
Wellsir, he pours hisself a drink, pours me

One too, 'n' I think, Lawd don't let it be
Like them bad days befo' when he 'uz racin'.
Well, he's sittin' there, jes' starin' at that

Bottle settin' restin' on the table, talkin'
At me, 'cept I knew it wadn't me
He's talkin' to. Nawsir, he 'uz

Talkin' ta the Lawd, wond'rin' why,
When he 'uz wild 'n' bad 'n' had that crash,
The Lawd, who shoulda sent his soul ta Satan,

Turned him round 'n' brought him back with that
Sweet vision boilin' in his head—the Lawd
Did that, but when it come ta Becca in the

Wreck, the Lawd done fetched her home, caught her
To His bosom, leavin' Bobby on his
Own 'n' those two boys without a ma.

Well, he kept on talkin' that way till ol'
Slim jes' had ta speak up fo' the Lawd.
I tol' him that the Lawd'd got His reasons,

'N' they's bigger by a heap then what
Men got. That's 'cause the Lawd done seen the end
A things ta come, 'n' knew how they got started too.

'Sides, I told him, once the Lawd'd
Chose him as His own to preach the Word,
Why he 'uz in fo' loads a trouble, loads a

Testin', so he'd best ta quit that aksin' why
'N' get ta carin' fo' them boys
That lost their ma 'n' fo' that little gal

That lost 'em both. That's what I tol' him, Mr. Print,
Durin' that whole evenin' we 'uz
Sittin' there. Then finally Bobby picks that

Shot glass full a whiskey up 'n' pours it
Down his throat in one big swalla. Well, I
Thought, sure 'nough, we 'uz done fo' then,

But then the boy jes' put the cork
Back in the bottle, whacked it with his hand
'N' dropped the bottle in the trash, then looks

At me 'n' says, "Slim, you rascal, what we
Sittin' here fo', we's got kids ta raise?"
That's when I cast my eyes ta heaven, shoutin'

In my head, "Hallelujah! The Lawd
Jehovah He jes' reached His hand down here
'N' touched the boy again!" 'N' then I picked

That shot glass full a sippin' whiskey up
'N' poured it down my throat, 'n' let me tell ya,
Mr. Charlie, that's the sweetest drink

A whiskey ol' Slim Daniels ever took.

CHARLIE: Yeah, Slim, that's all OK, but what's that got
Ta do with Nick 'n' Bubba's fallin' out?

SLIM: Well, Mr. Print, that's where it all began.
Seems the minute they were born, their Momma
Favored Nicky more. 'N' when they's growin' up,

Why, he'd be always laughin', playin' tricks.
Once, when I 'uz dozin' in a rocker,
Nicky give ol' Uncle Slim the hot foot.

Well now, I wakes up snap! 'n' sees my shoe
On fire 'n' foot! I knows what rascal done that.
Jumpin' 'n' hoppin' 'n' stompin', I chased him down,

Jes' about ta whale the dickens from
His backside when his Momma come along
'N' saved him from a lickin', sayin', "Be sweet,

Nicky, tell your Uncle Slim you didn't
Mean it." So that's jes' what he says, like butter
Wouldn't melt there in his mouth, but, say,

If that boy meant it, Mr. Print, I'll eat
A bug, 'cause he goes walkin' off, a-holdin'
His Momma's hand 'n' turns 'n' gives ol' Slim

A look a pure-D devilment. Wellsir,
With Nicky bein' Becca's fav'rite child,
Seem natch'ly Bobby took ta Jess, 'n' look here,

That boy aimed ta please. Tried ta know each
Thing his daddy wanted 'fo' he said it.
Then when Becca died, that's when Nicky

Saw that he'd be always second best with Bobby,
Suckin' hind tit like they say.
'N' when his Pa adopted Donna, 'swhen he

Dropped ta number three. Seemed ta think the
Only way ta get his pa's attention
'Uz by cuttin' up, misbehavin'

(The way he mos'ly got his Ma ta spoil him).
All them teenage years, why, he 'uz in 'n'
Out a scrapes, jes' tryin' see 'ud Bobby

Pay some mind. But then when Nick 'uz in his
Twenties, Bobby'd got sa tired a that boy's
Stunts 'n' figurin' why he pulled 'em, seems he'd

Jes' ignore 'em. That's when Nicky cooked up
Somethin' big, somethin' Bobby never'd
Turn his back on—that rascal started courtin'

Donna, talkin' how they 'uz gonna get
Engaged, that Nicky'd loved her since they both
'Uz kids.

CHARLIE: So that's the straw hat broke the camel's

Back.

SLIM: Don't know about no camels, Mr.
Print, but that's sure 'nough what made his daddy
Set his face agin him. They had this great

Big fight, almost came ta blows, 'n' Bobby
Ran him off, then Bobby called the folks
Together from the show 'n' told 'em how he'd

Jes' disowned this Nicky Elray, cast him
From his sight, 'n' none a them 'ud best be
Seen with Nicky now, or they'd be cast off too.

CHARLIE: Wha'did Donna say ta that?
SLIM: Wellsir, ya know young Donna thinks the sun
           Jes' rises up 'n' sets in her ol' Uncle

Bobby, so when Bobby put the hex on
Nicky, she 'uz caught there 'tween the man's
Been like a daddy to her ev'ry since

She's been a sprout 'n' that fun-lovin' rascal
Always actin' like the older brother.
Come to that other kinda love, that's Nick's

Imagination cookin' somethin' up the boy
Could tie ta Bobby's tail jes' like
Some ol' tin can.

CHARLIE: Ya sure 'bout that one, Slim?

Ev'ry time I saw the twins 'n' Donna
Pallin' 'round, she always seemed right partial
Where young Nick's concerned, 'n' 'peared ta me

She wouldn't give young Jess the time a day.
SLIM: Nawsir, I don't believe there's nothin' 'tween
           Them two like that. But yonder comes the gal—

Aks her fo' yourself. Miss Donna, darlin',
Look who I got here with me.

(*An attractive young woman in her mid-twenties enters
stage left. She has the sunny, energetic disposition of a
believer but also a sharp sense of humor.*)

DONNA: Why, Uncle
Slim, I heard from Bubba Mr. Print 'ud

Be here. How're ya doin', Mr. Printwhistle?

CHARLIE: Donna, I believe you must get prettier
Ev'ry time I see ya.

DONNA: Why, Mr. Charlie,

You're just sayin' that 'cause it's true.

CHARLIE: 'N' snippy as ever, seems to me.

DONNA: Wouldn't
Be me if it wadn't. 'Sides I didn't have

No sayso how I look, that's all the Lord's
Own work 'n' like the lilies of the field
That neither toil or spin, the beauty a this here

World jes' serves ta magnify the Lord.
But 'scuse me for a minute, Mr. Print.
Uncle Slim, Jesse asked could you

Come down 'n' help him with the deacons. No one's
Good as you, he says, at puttin' deacons
Through close-order drill, preparin' for the

Basket-passin'.

SLIM: Yessum, got ta keep
Them boys in line, got ta see that some
Big wind don't come up sudden, blow them dollar

Bills right off the basket tops 'n' inta
Those boys' pockets, 'fo' they gets the baskets
Back 'n' we can count 'em. So I believe

I'll say good-bye now, Mr. Print. See ya
After all the shoutin's done, up ta Bobby's
Room at that hotel.

CHARLIE: So long,

See ya later. (*Slim exits.*)
    That ol' fella's a caution.

DONNA: Yes, sir, he's a treasure.

CHARLIE: He sure does think
The world a Bubba.

DONNA: Uncle Bubba says

If ever he gets through heaven's door, first thing
He's gonna do is look around for Slim,
'N' if there's some mistake 'n' Slim's not there,

Bubba says he dudn't think he'll stay.
Uncle Slim tell ya 'bout the time
Bubba cussed him, called ol' Slim a loser?

CHARLIE: Yeah.

DONNA: How many times ya heard that story,
Mr. Charlie?

CHARLIE: Over the years,
Two, three times I guess.

DONNA: Uncle Bubba

Says that's how the Lord'd planned ta punish
Him for sayin' that mean thing ta Slim—
Havin' Slim tell ev'ryone that Bubba

Knows, or's ever gonna, what he said.

CHARLIE: Ev'ry time he tells it though,
He still forgives him at the end.

DONNA: Uncle

Bubba says he's waitin' for the time when
Slim gets tired a tellin' it
That same ol' way, maybe then he'll change the ending,

Make it a surprise, then Bubba says
Slim'll realize the reason he's
Been tellin' it for years ta anyone 'ud

Listen's 'cause, deep down inside, he never
Did forgive him, dontcha know?

CHARLIE: Maybe so.
Slim 'n' me's jes' talkin' 'bout

How Nicky musta been that second caller
On the show today.

DONNA: That boy! Ever
Since the bust-up, dev'lin' Bubba's been

The grits he eats for breakfast.

CHARLIE: Ya know, when Nicky
Started talkin', he disguised his voice,
Sounded like the kinda sad sack usu'lly

Calls for free advice most times when there's
A preacher on the show, but once that rascal
Had ol' Bubba hooked 'n' talkin', why,

His put-on voice changed with ev'ry word.
I could tell from Bubba's face
He recognized the caller, 'swhy he cut him off

Sa quick.

DONNA: That figures. Growin' up, Nick could
Imitate 'most anybody's voice,
'Specially Jesse's. 'Member how their mother

Used ta dress the boys alike as kids—
Well, that's when Nick 'ud tease his daddy 'cause he
Figured Bubba'd always favored Jess.

Times he'd wait till Jess was off somewheres,
Then Nick 'ud find his pa, pretendin' he's
His brother. A course, he had the voice 'n' all

Down pat, but what 'ud fool his pa 'most ev'ry
Time 'uz Nick'd butter up his daddy
Sumthin' fierce jes' like Jesse did.

CHARLIE: Dudn't seem like that's changed much?
DONNA:
                                            Not a bit.
             Wellsir, after the first few times
             A him pretendin' he was Jesse, Nick felt sure

             What he'd suspicioned 'bout his Pa.
             Next thing ya know, soon as Nicky pulled
             That stunt again 'n' Bubba took the bait,

             Sayin' somethin' provin' Jess 'uz Bubba's
             Fav'rite, Nicky laughed in Bubba's face 'n'
             Ran away, callin' back sidewise

             'Cross his shoulder, "Yeah, but, Daddy, I'm
             Not Jess, I'm Nick." Well, let me tell ya, Mr. Print,
             Seems like that trick left Uncle Bubba

             Plumb bumfuzzled. Times when Jesse'd be
             Alone with Bubba after that, his daddy'd
             Kinda keep him at a distance, starin'

             At his face, seein' could he tell
             If it was Nick playactin'. Well, a course,
             Jesse didn't know what he'd done wrong,

             'N' Bubba wadn't 'bout to tell him how his
             Brother'd fooled him, so the only thing
             Jesse knew ta do was suck up even

More, till even Bubba got uneasy,
Thinkin' maybe it was Nicky
Cookin' up another stunt. Well, Jesse

Finally figured out what Nick'd done,
But only 'cause his brother told him one day
Out a spite. They were wranglin' over

Somethin', Jess was actin' uppity like he
Always does, like he's his daddy's right-hand
Man, so Nicky thought he'd take him down

A peg, 'n' spilled the beans.

CHARLIE: What did Jesse
Say ta that?

DONNA: He said since he forgave him,
So would God—like Jesse wadn't only

Bubba's right-hand man but slept inside
The Lord's coat pocket too.

CHARLIE: Yeah, I've heard him
Talk that way ta folks.

DONNA: Well, ya know,

Mr. Charlie, after Aunt Rebecca
Died, the two boys never dressed alike
Again, 'cept for once. They musta been

Fifteen, Jess was off somewhere, so Nicky
Got in Jesse's room 'n' put his brother's
Clothes on. Soon as he was dressed, what else

But he goes lookin' for his pa, pretendin'
He's his brother. Wellsir, seems that Uncle
Bubba felt real low that day, missin'

Becca somethin' awful, so he opens up,
Sayin' what a comfort Jesse'd
Been, someone close who understood

His pain 'n' tried to hep him any way
He could. Well, who knows how, maybe jes'
An eyebrow kinda risin', his lip jes' startin' in

Ta curl, but Bubba all uva sudden
Sees it's not young Jesse's face he's lookin'
Inta there but Nick's. Well, Mr. Charlie,

Bubba gets sa mad, he slaps him right
Across the mouth, slaps him hard. Nicky's
Standin' there, tears puddlin' in his eyes

'Fore he says, "Think you're the only one
That misses Momma?"

CHARLIE: Wha'did Bubba say ta that?
DONNA: Uncle Bubba started in

Apologizin', said he shouldn'ta lost
His temper, struck his son in anger. Nick
Jes' turned his back 'n' walked away, like his

Daddy weren't no more ta him than spit.
Well, Uncle Bubba musta told on Nick
'Cause after that Jesse locked his bedroom

Door whenever he went out.

CHARLIE: Did Jess
Raise hell with Nicky, borrowin' his clothes?
DONNA: You must be funnin', Mr. Print. Ever

Since the two a them were kids, if Jesse'd
Got a bone ta pick with Nick, he'd pipe
Right up, till Nick 'ud smile 'n' say, "Zat so?,"

Lookin' kinda thoughtful, dontcha know?,
Then murmur, "I'll sure think on it, but look here
In the meantime you consider this,"

Then sidle up ta Jess 'n' punch him hard
Right in the belly. Time they'd turned
Fifteen, that happened often enough young

Jesse didn't mess with Nick at all.
But seems ta me from then on Jesse's suckin' up
'Stead a bein' just a way

A gettin' more affection from his Pa,
Somethin' makin' up, dontcha see?,
For what he felt he missed by Becca idolizin'

Nick, turned more 'n' more as time went on
To some mean plan, freezin' Nicky out,
Keepin' him from any share in Uncle

Bubba's pulpit, havin' any sayso
'Bout the family business. Guess
You've heard a this Pure Products of America?

Well, Uncle Bubba had the idea first,
Then Jesse organized the whole shebang—
Incorporated, up in Delaware.

He runs it now. He's the one jest hired
That hotshot 'ccountant fella usedta work
Down there at Enron. After that he put

The TV deal together, spreadin' Uncle
Bubba's preachin' 'cross the South. Next thing ya know,
He's goin' national, then it's Europe.

Each new move, more sayso ends up
Stickin' to his fingers. When Nick was still around,
We stuck together jes' ta keep from bein'

Bulldozed. That's when Nicky got the idea
Maybe there was more between us two than
Bein' raised together, more than cousins

Holdin' close for self-protection. 'Swhen
He said that silly thing about us gettin'
Hitched made his daddy hit the ceilin'.

Now it's Jesse this 'n' Jesse that—
With a finger in ev'ry blesséd pie.
Lord a mighty! Speak a the devil!

(*A young man enters briskly from stage left, walking as
if he owned the building. He walks right through Donna
to get to Charlie Printwhistle and holds out his hand.*)

JESSE: Mr.

Charlie, daddy said you'd be backstage
Tonight, I just wanted ta say how much we
All appreciate that interview today,

Even with that smart-mouthed second caller.

CHARLIE: I was tellin' Donna sounded
Like it might be Nick.

JESSE: Wouldn't put it

Past him for a minute. Donna, 'bout time
You were crankin' up the choir, idn't it?
'Member that director fella wants 'em

Goin' flat out when he cues the fade-in
For the show.

DONNA: Think I maybe knew that, Jesse,
Seein's I've only done it start a

Ev'ry blesséd TV program Uncle
Bubba's had. Well, Mr. Charlie, gotta
Get ta work. Will I see ya after?

CHARLIE: I'm stayin' for the start a Bubba's sermon,
Donna, but I gotta run an errand, so I'll
Catch ya both up later back at Ace's

Hotel suite.
(*Donna exits.*)

JESSE: Mr. Charlie,
I'm glad we got this chance ta jaw some by
Ourselves.

CHARLIE: What's on your mind, Jesse?

JESSE: Daddy

Told me you all talked about Pure Products,
Right? Wellsir, I been linin' up
Some folks, ones with local visibility,

Dontcha know?, folks with media access,
Celebrities 'n' such, seein' how they'd
Play as regional spokesmen for Pure Products.

Way we'd work's a lot like Amway. You'd
Recruit five representatives-slash-salesmen, see?,
Then each a them recruit five more 'n'

So on, right on down the line. It's like
A pyramid, with you there at the top.
Ev'ry time the boys below ya make a

Sale, you get a cut, 'cause you're the regional
Spokesman. Maybe mention couple a times
A day on air how much ya like Pure Products,

Right?

(*The sound of singing begins in the auditorium off
stage.*)

There goes Donna 'n' the choir.

CHARLIE: My, that little gal sure can sing.

JESSE: Daddy says that's what the angels sound like,

Mr. Print. So whatcha think about
This regional spokesman deal?

CHARLIE: Got somethin' written
Down y'all could send me, set the terms?

JESSE: Sure do. I'll have my people send it ta
Your people.

CHARLIE: Hell, Jesse, I ain't got
No people, have 'em send it jes' ta me—

Over ta the station.

JESSE: Will do, Mr. Charlie.
Here comes Daddy now. He always hits
The boards soon's the choir starts in singin'.

(*Bubba enters, holding out his hand to Charlie.*)

BUBBA: Charlie, how ya doin'? Slim'd told me
You were down here countin' heads.

CHARLIE: Nawsir,
I'se jes' jawin' here with Jesse, 'spectin'

Any time the big Kahuna'd be upon us.

BUBBA: How we fixed for time?

JESSE: Minute or so,

Daddy, 'fore I introduce ya.

Choir's 'bout half way through "Ol' Rugged Cross."

BUBBA: Jesse tell ya what he had in mind here, Charlie,

'Bout you bein' regional spokesman?

CHARLIE: Sure did, Ace. Talked jes' now.

BUBBA: Whatcha think?

CHARLIE: Well, like I told young Jesse, send some paperwork

'N' let me think on it real hard.

BUBBA: Like the hymn says, Print, "that's good enough

Fer me." Jess, 'bout time you got on stage

'N' kicked things off.

JESSE: Yes, sir.

(Jesse exits right.)

BUBBA: Gonna stay

Ta see the whole show, Charlie?

CHARLIE: Like to, Ace,

But look, I gotta run an errand so I'll

Stay ta hear your sermonizin' whip 'em

To a frenzy, then I'll catch ya up some later

Back ta your hotel.

BUBBA: You're a

Heathen from a long line a heathens, Print,

But jes' you mark my words, I'm gonna

Save that soul a yours some day 'spite a

Your best efforts.

CHARLIE: Good luck, Ace.

*(From stage right, the choir finishes singing and we hear
Jesse's voice.)*

JESSE: Thank ya,

Choir, for that soul-stirrin' hymn, 'n' now
The moment you good folks been hank'rin' for,
That four-square gospel preacher, prophet, pilgrim—

Rev'rend Ray Bob Elray, daddy ta me
But brother in the Lord ta ev'ryone a
You come here tonight.

BUBBA: That's my cue.
(Bubba starts walking off stage right.)

CHARLIE: Break

A leg, Bubba.

BUBBA: Heathen!

*(Bubba exits stage right; a moment later Jesse enters
stage right. From stage right comes the sound of the
crowd on seeing Bubba, a general sigh of satisfaction
mingled with "Amens!" and "Hallelujahs!")*

                              Brothers 'n' sisters,
My text tonight is Luke 15:11 ta
32, fer all you folks brought along

Your bibles. Story 'bout a man
Had two sons, a parable the good Lord
Tells them Pharisees 'n' scribes (that's like

Your lawyers 'n' your court reporters now'days).
Seems them Pharisees 'n' scribes been jawin'
On the Lord 'bout how He hung around

With sinners, so he tells 'em this here story
Jes' ta twist their tails a might? Seems one a
This man's sons pipes up 'n' says, "Daddy,

I'm a-hankerin' ta travel, why dontcha
Gimme my inheritance upfront?"
Well now, this pappy loved his boys 'n' so,

Sure 'nough, that's jes' the thing he did, divided
Up his substance, gave the younger son
His portion, like the Good Book says. This boy

Goes travelin', dontcha know?—rodeoin',
Bronc-ridin', calf-ropin'—livin' wild 'n' wastin'
All his substance till he wakes up in

An alley some ol' early mornin', empty
Pint stuck in a paper sack a-layin'
On his chest, dried-up vomit on his

Shirt, 'n' not a nickel in his jeans,
With that cat-furry taste there in his mouth—
Boy-howdy! I can see there in your eyes

Some a you ol' boys know jes' the thing
I'm talkin' 'bout—well now, this fella's layin'
There, a-lickin' uv his lips, movin'

His jaw real gentle with his fingers, testin'
Is it broke ('cause someone slugged him in
A honky-tonk last night), jes' seein' can he

Talk, speak one word, 'n' what's that word?
You guessed it, folks, the boy says, "Daddy, hep me."
Hooee! Quick as that! The boy's a-walkin'

Toward the freight yards, hops a boxcar, walks them
Last few weary miles along that dirt road
Runs upside his father's spread 'n' what's

He see? His pappy out on horseback ridin'
Fence, well, soon's his daddy see'd him comin'
Up the road, he gives a whoop, his son

Come runnin', sayin' "Daddy, I done sinned
Against high heaven, 'n' you ta boot—till I
Ain't worthy no how bein' called your son."

But, folks, you think that daddy gave a hoot
About all that? Why, he just hugged his neck
'N' kissed his cheek 'n' called his ranch hands out

A-sayin', "Let my son here get a wash-up
In the tank ('cause he's nigh smellin' like
A goat!), then fetch the boy fresh duds 'n' my

New pair a boots, 'n' kill that fatted calf
'Cause we're a-headed fer a barbecue.
My son was dead, but he's alive again,

Was lost but now he's found." Then all them ranch hands
Raised a hooraw big enough the rancher's
Elder son come ridin' up 'n' see'd

What's what 'n' got plumb angry, sayin', "Daddy,
All these years I worked the ranch, rode
The range, 'n' done what's right, you never killed

No calf for me. Yet here you done it fer
My brother Dusty after he done misbehaved
'N' wasted all his substance. That ain't

Right." Well now, you know, folks, that ol' daddy
He loved both his boys 'n' so he smiles 'n'
Tells the elder, "Rusty, thou art ever

With me, son, 'n' all I have is thine,
But it was sure 'nough meet that we make merry,
Fer thy brother that was dead's alive again,

Was lost but now is found." That's what
The good Lord told them Pharisees 'n' scribes,
But notice in your Bibles, folks, that son

When he returned, abased hisself before
His pa, confessed his faults 'n' then repented,
That's the reason his dear daddy took him back.

But 'spose when Dusty woke up in that
Alley 'stead a hoppin' on a fast freight
Headin' home, he'd mosey'd down the alley,

Found another cowboy passed out, rolled him
Fer his poke, then started honky-tonkin' hard
Till 'long 'bout three A.M. young Dusty

Ends up drunk inside a phone booth, callin'
Home. Well, folks, that phone starts ringin' in his
Daddy's bedroom, dontcha know?, ringin'

Till his pappy tumbles out a bed,
Blinkin' 'n' blank, long johns 'n' ol' sockfeet,
Standin' there a-sayin', "Hello? Hello?"

'Cause no one answers, then his pa says, "Dusty,
That you, son?"—still nothin', so he goes on
"Son, don't be ashamed, it's jes' your Pa

That loves ya, boy. Tell me whatcha want 'n'
Where ya are." A pause, 'n' then he hears that
Drunken son-in-a-booth a-buzzin' his big,

Pink tongue in daddy's ear, jes' givin' pap
The razzberry, dontcha know? Well now, I ask
You folks, what's the good Lord think a father's

'Sposed ta do a-facin' trashy conduct
From a son phones up at three A.M.?

CHARLIE: I think I know where this is headed, Jess.

I'll catch ya up some later back at that hotel.

(*Charlie exits, stage left, as Bubba's voice resumes from stage right.*)

BUBBA: 'Cause ya know, Lord God Jehovah He's
A daddy, biggest daddy uv 'em all.

Whatchu think He'd do some bad boy phoned him
Three A.M., woke him up, then buzzed
His tongue jes' like a fart. Why, folks,

Ya know the Lord Jehovah he'd be right
In fillin' that boy's phone booth full a cow flop,
Packin' that boy's shorts with them red fire ants,

Jeans with stingin' nettles, He'd be justified
I say, but that ain't what He wants,
Our Lord's a God a mercy, all's He asks is

Zat boy come on back 'n' tell his pa,
"Daddy, you was right 'n' I was wrong,
'N' I ain't fit no more ta be your son."

That's all He asks, 'n' then He'd say, "Boys, throw
A rope around that fatted calf, 'n' git
That charcoal fire a-goin'." 'Cause like the good Lord

Says, there's more rejoicin' up in heaven
Fer that lost sheep when it's found than fer
The ninety-nine's never strayed, 'n' more

Hoorawin' fer the dead son once he's come back
Home, than fer that good son never sowed
Wild oats ta start with, seems.

JESSE: Yeah, right, ol' man!

Act One

(*The living room of Big Bubba's hotel suite later on the same night as act 1, scene 2. An insistent knocking is heard on the hotel room door. Slim Daniels enters from the bedroom, stage right. The knocking resumes.*)

SLIM: Hold on, I'm comin'. (*Opens door.*) Hey there, Mr. Charlie.

CHARLIE: How ya doin', Slim? (*Looks around.*) Where's ev'rybody at? Thought sure they'd be back home by now.

SLIM: Nawsir, big excitement likely
Held 'em up. What time d'ya leave the hall
This evenin'?

CHARLIE: Bubba'd jes' got on his hind legs

Speechifyin'.

SLIM: Wellsir, after that
The choir gals sang, 'n' Donna jes' like always
Had her solo, that's when Bobby called on those

Afflicted with the mis'ry there ta
Come right up on stage 'n' get the layin'
On a hands. But jes' 'tween you 'n' me,

Mr. Charlie, right before the service started,
We'd aksed them 'fflicted folks, the ones'd
Showed up fer the healin', could they raise

Their hands up, so's the deacons walkin' through
The hall could check 'em out, frisk 'em maybe.
Done that since this Rice boy down in Houston

Couple weeks ago'd slipped this big ol'
Rubber bladder filled with pee up underneath
His coat, jes' like he 'uz a humpback,

Dontcha know? Well, Lawd a mercy, Mr. Print,
When Bobby whacked that rascal's forehead,
Shoutin' out, "Be gone, thou unclean spirit,"

That young satan fell down flat like he 'uz
Poleaxed, messed hisself right there, a-stretched out
On the floor.

CHARLIE: Yeah, Slim, Bubba told me all

About it. Said them Rice boys in
The balcony commenced ta makin' fartin'
Noises with there tongues, askin' why

He didn't part the Yellow Sea like Moses.
SLIM: Yessuh, they sure 'nough did—bunch a bad uns,
Rotten ta the bone. But that's why Bobby

Tol' the deacons ev'ry since, "Jes' put
The squinch eye on them folks that come up
Fer the healin'." Wellsir, all this batch

Checked out. First one up's a young man walkin'
Kinda funny, shaky-legged, jerkin'
All around, bobbin' back 'n' forth.

Jes' one look 'n' Dr. Slim done diagnosed
This fella's 'ffliction where he stood:
Clearest case a ol' St. Virus dance

Ya ever seen. Now Bobby, as a rule,
Likes startin' with the hard uns, that's the reason
Shaky-leg 'uz first, 'n' while this fella's

Walkin' 'cross the stage, Bobby rushes
At him, grabs the fella's shoulders, pullin'
Him up straight 'n' shoutin' in his face,

"Do you believe?" Well now, the boy
'Uz startled, scared in front a all them folks, ya see,
So all he manages to say's

This weak, "I do." Well, Bobby knew that wadn't
Near belief enough ta get the healin'
Goin', so he put his face up close

'N' shouted in his ear, "DO YOU BELIEVE?"
'N' then the boy, why, he jes' shouted back,
"YES, JESUS! YES, I DO!" Well, they went back

'N' forth like that, gettin' louder, maybe
Two, three times, till that boy's face got red
'N' he's a-shoutin' like his head's about ta

Pop. Then Bobby stops him short 'n' lookin'
In his eyes, he says, "Be gone, thou shaky demon"—
Well, Bobby had aholt a this boy's shoulders still

'N' starts right in a-shakin' him,
Like some ol' rag doll. Recollect, Mr. Print,
My Bobby started out a wrestler 'fore

He turned ta grapplin' with the devil.
So when it comes ta fixin' folks, why, he can
Shake 'em worse 'n any dry martini

Back in his drinkin' days. So I was watchin'
From the wings when that boy's eyes like
Angry marbles got ta bouncin' in

His head, then Bobby give him one last shake,
Snapped his head back good, that's when the fella's
Eyeballs rolled right up inside his skull.

Then Bobby turned him loose 'n' down he dropped,
Smack dab! right on his knees, lookin' like he's
Gonna keel right over, seems, but Bobby's

Always got two deacons standin' by,
'N' these boys caught that 'fflicted fella underneath
The arms, snatched him up, 'n' held him

High, straight up on his tiptoes, see,
'N' as he's sorta fallin' forward, why,
The fella takes a step or two, lookin almos'

Natch'al. Bobby shouts, "Praise Jesus!," well,
The crowd starts shoutin' too, 'n' Bobby puts
His face up close, a-whisperin' at the boy,

"Say it. Say, 'Praise Jesus!'" But the boy's
So stunned from all the shakin', why, the fella
Can't say boo, till Bobby starts to raise

His arms up towards his shoulders, like he's aimin'
Fer another shake, 'n' that boy shouts, "Oh God!
Praise Jesus!," when Bobby gives the deacons there

A sign 'n' they quick-step this pilgrim off the stage,
Kinda ballet-dancin' on his tiptoes.
Next one up's this teenage gal,

Says she always sad 'n' mos' time always cryin',
Jes' can't stop. So Bobby aks her,
What she cryin' fer. The gal says she

Don't know—mus' be 'cause she's sad. So Bobby
Aks her if she 'cepts the Lawd Jehovah's
Son as her own pers'nal savior. Yes,

She says, real meek. So then he aks her, does she
Recollect how Jesus let the soldiers
Put them nails plumb through his hands 'n' feet,

'N' how he wore that thorny crown, then let 'em
Poke that spear up in his side—'n' all
Account a this gal's sins. So she says yes again,

'N' starts ta cry, the tears jes' rollin'
Down her cheeks, so Bobby takes her face
In both his hands, a-sayin' real gentle, "Sister,

Dontcha know how Jesus loves ya? Dontcha
Know the Lawd don't wantcha sad? But if
He give ya this affliction, there's a reason.

Maybe Jesus means ta let ya know, when you
Get blue, how bad He felt a-hangin'
On the cross, or make ya think, if tears

Go pourin' down your cheeks, a them ol' bloody
Drops a-rainin' down His face from that
Sharp crown, so, sis, right there's the cure fer your

Affliction: when you start feelin' sad 'n' start
Ta cry, why, you're not suff'rin' helpless, no.
'Cause now you know the reason, know the Lawd

Done given you a special gift, a share
In Jesus' suff'rin', yes. So if them tears
Well up, you say, 'Yes, Jesus.' Second thought,

Jes' shout it out. Jes' shout, 'Yes, Jesus!'" Well, Mr. Print,
Seems this here batch uv 'fflicted folks was slow
On what they calls "the uptake," didn't

Know the portacall a Bobby's healin', no.
So this gal's standin' there a-sobbin',
Tryin' ta catch her breath, not sayin' nothin',

Looked like some ol' zombie. So my Bobby
Tries this trick he learnt back in them wrestlin'
Days, when some boy'd get knocked out. Way we'd

Bring 'em to's take aholt their earlobes,
Pull 'em hard, then pinch 'em good till they come 'round.
So that's what Bobby done, but first

He told this gal again, "Jes' say, 'Yes, Jesus.'"
Well, seems she couldn't say it fer the sobbin',
So he takes his hand, one that's restin'

On her cheek, offside from the crowd,
Grabs her ear 'n' twists it good 'n' hard
Till this gal shouts out, "YEEOW! JESUS!" Bobby

Says, "That's it. Yeeow, Jesus!," twistin'
It again until she shouts it even
Louder. Next the crowd starts shoutin' too,

"Yeeow, Jesus! Yeeow, Jesus!" Then he
Nods to them two deacons quick, 'n' this gal's
Arm-projected off the stage. 'N' as she's

Passin' by me, where I 'uz standin' 'hind
The curtain, still a-whimp'rin', rubbin' uv her ear,
I calls out, "Sister, now ya know

The kind a thing's worth cryin' 'bout." Well, next one up's
A redneck, real ol' country boy,
Bib overalls, blue work shirt, one brown hightop

Shoe, 'n' walkin' with a crutch, 'cause this here
Fella's other leg 'uz off below
The knee. But that tweren't his affliction, nawsir.

Deacons know ta keep them folks that's missin'
Uva limb from comin' up on stage.
That's not the kind a trade my Bobby

Handles. Seems this fella's 'ffliction was
A deefness in his ears, couldn't hardly
Hear when Bobby aks'd him did he 'ccept

Lord Jesus Christ to be his pers'nal savior.
Bobby had to get up close 'n' shout right
In his earhole. 'Swhen this ol' boy yells,

"Yes, preacher! Yes, I do!" Well, Bobby has
This little bag a dirt he always carries
In his pocket fer occasions jes' like this.

So now he pours some dirt out in his hand,
Mixes it with spit ta make
A paste, then plugs it good 'n' tight in this

Boy's ears. Well, this ol' cracker's lookin' mighty
Doubtful, seein' how the preacher done packed
Mud 'n' spit there in his earholes, but

He figures, if ya don't have faith, can't nothin'
Good come out. So that's when Bobby puts
His hands six inches either side the fella's

Head 'n' says, "Euphrates! Be thou open!"
Then smacks his hands, hard's he can, right smart
Against the fella's ears. Well, Mr. Print,

Ya know, we mos' times keeps a room backstage
Fer folks that's overcome by Bobby's preachin',
So I knew then jes' where this boy 'uz headed

Once the deacons scooped him off the floor.
Well now, a couple more a them afflicted
Folk come through, 'n' then the healin' part the show's

Mos' done, so Bobby cued the choir ta
Make a joyful noise befo' the Lawd
'N' dance around the tabernacle. Bobby

Alwayst joins the dancin', 'cause, ya know,
That boy is jes' a cloggin' fool mos' any time
He hears his favorite hymn "Great Gettin'-Up

Mornin.'" Well, his arms 'n' legs are goin'
All which ways, robe a-flyin' back 'n' forth
Jes' like them stormy waves, 'n' then he starts

Ta speak in tongues—"A-willa-willa-wally-
Wooly-wooly-woo"—when all at once
From out the wings, way 'cross the stage, that country

Boy who'd lost his leg comes leapin', mud 'n'
Spit a-dribblin' from his ears, but Lawd!
He's standin' on two feet 'n' shoutin',

"I can hear! Praise Jesus! I can dance!"
'N' sure enough, one shoe on 'n' one
Shoe off, the boy begins ta clog like I ain't

Never seen nobody dance befo'.
Well, let me tell ya, Mr. Print, this time
My Bobby was the one them deacons had ta

Pick up off the floor. The crowd commenced
Ta shoutin', gals a-singin' in the choir
Commenced ta faintin', folks fell down right on

Their knees, tears a-streamin' down their cheeks—
It was pandemonium, Mr. Print,
Pan-demonium. Well, that cable TV

Show still had a couple a minutes ta go,
So Jesse come a-runnin' out on stage
'N' put hisself smack dab in front the camera,

Smilin', thankin' everybody, tryin'
Could he give his daddy time ta pull
Hisself together 'fore the close,

When all uva sudden that ol' country boy
Come cloggin' up ta Jesse, grabs him by
The hand, 'n' pulls him back to where my Bobby's

Standin' with the deacons, tryin' ta catch
His breath. Wellsir, he grabs aholt a Bobby's
Hand 'n' now he's got young Jesse on

His left 'n' Bobby on his right, 'n' this ol'
Country boy's a-cloggin' like a dancin' fool,
Shoutin' "I can hear, Lawd! I can

Dance!" The crowd's a-goin wild, so Bobby
Takes one look 'n' starts in cloggin' fast's he can,
Jes' keepin' up with that ol' country

Boy. Well, natch'ly, Jesse's got ta start in
Too, so there's the three a them, hand in
Hand, center stage, jes' cloggin' fit

Ta beat the band while folks out front're whoopin'
'N' hollerin', singin' 'n' sobbin', Mr. Print.
That's when the TV camera moves in fer a

Close-up on them three 'n' *snap!* the show 'uz done.
Wellsir, let me tell ya, tryin' ta
Get them folks calmed down was sure 'nough gonna

Be a job a work, so Bobby tol' me
Come on back 'n' let you in 'n' say
Soon's he'd finished up he'd be back thisaways

Directly. So whatcha think now, Mr. Print?
The Lord Jehovah he done reached
His hand down here again ta signify

His favor for his prophet, cured that fella's
Leg ta show my Bobby stands in tight there
With the Lawd.

CHARLIE: Well, Slim, I'd sure 'nough like

Ta see that leg before I take a stand on it.
Back in them olden days that sorta
Thing 'ud happen all the time, but now'days

Not so much. 'Course, I hear tell Eye-talians
Still believe the good Saint Anthony
Once reattached a fella's foot. Seems one day

This fella got upset, 'n' whatcha know?,
He hauled right off 'n' kicked his momma down
The stairs, so when the saint got wind a this,

He went 'n' tol' this youngster, "Any boy 'ud
Kick his mother don't deserve ta have
A foot." That's when this fella went on home

'N' took an axe 'n' whacked the guilty trotter off
Up close. First thing ya know here comes
His ma a-lookin' fer the saint, a-sayin'

'Cause a what he tol' her boy he better
Come right quick 'n' put that foot back on.
Well 'course, the good Saint Anthony done jes'

The thing she asked. But seems I recollect
That foot was layin' 'round the house somewhere
Jes' waitin' fer the saint, where I don't figure

That ol' country boy that Bubba healed
Had brought along a spare leg toted in a
Tow sack jes' in case ol' Ace'd got

His game face on that day. Nawsir, Slim,
I think there's somethin' fishy goin' on.

SLIM: It's like my Bobby says, Mr. Print,

You's a heathen from a long ol' line
A heathens, ready ta put the stink eye on the
Lawd's own work come any chance ya get.

(*A sound at the hotel room door and Bubba, Donna, and
Jesse enter.*)

CHARLIE: Well, here he is, the man a the hour. Hear you
                Been out raisin' the dead or some such stunt.
BUBBA: How ya doin', Charlie.
SLIM: Bobby, he's been

                Sayin' things like that, makin' fun
                A miracles 'n' jawin' on the Lawd.
BUBBA: Slim, dontcha know?, Print likes ta play the devil's

                Advocate. Don't pay the man no nevermind.
SLIM: Bein' it's Mr. Print I knew
                The devil had ta be mixed up there somewhere.

DONNA: Mr. Print, ya sure did miss a grand
                Occasion. Never saw the Spirit movin'
                In a crowd the way it was tonight.

CHARLIE: Slim tol' me all about it, Donna. How
                The cloggin' a that one-legged-boy-that-was
                Had got'em faintin' in the choir 'n' floppin'

                In the aisles. Better than fireworks on the Fourth.
SLIM: Bobby, there he goes again!
                Jes' give a nod, 'n' lemme run him off.

BUBBA: Naw, Slim, it's like the Good Book says, Whenever
                The unbeliever scorns ya to your face,
                Return him good for evil, 'cause that way

                You'll be a-heapin' coals a fire upon his head.
CHARLIE: Yeah, Slim, ya know, it's like that hot foot
                Nicky gave ya years ago—jes' upside down.

SLIM:	Please, Bobby, lemme run him off.
JESSE:	Mr. Print, I do believe the Lord Was present in that hall tonight.
CHARLIE:	Well, that's

All well 'n' good, but I jes' hope ya got
That country boy that Bubba healed
Under lock 'n' key somewhere 'cause come tomorrow

Lotsa folks are gonna want ta pull
That fella's leg ta see if Bubba's pullin'
Theirs.

JESSE: I left him with two deacons, holdin'

On his arms 'n' told 'em, "Put him up
In some motel, then go get him in the mornin.'"
Well, I know it's kinda late

But mos' times when the show is done, we go on
Out 'n' have a meal. Ya care ta join us,
Mr. Charlie.

CHARLIE: Don't mind if I do,

That's if Bubba don't mind bein' seen
Out drinkin' with a sinner.

BUBBA: Charlie, I ain't
Touched a drop in years, you know that.

'Sides the fact any harm my reputation 'ud
Take from bein' seen consortin' with a
Heathen's done been suffered long ago.

But Jesse, you 'n' Slim 'n' Donna
Go on down 'n' see if they're still servin'.
If they are, ya know the thing I'd order.

JESSE:

Me 'n' Print'll be down there directly.
I jes' want ta jaw a spell with him some.
All right, Daddy. See ya in a minute.

DONNA:

See ya, Mr. Print.

SLIM:

Bobby, if he
Starts ta raggin' on the Lawd, jes' pick
That phone up, I'll come back 'n' run him off.

BUBBA:

I can handle Charlie, Slim. See ya
In a minute.
(*Exit Jesse, Donna, and Slim.*)

CHARLIE:

What's up, Bubba?

BUBBA:

Print,
I don't know what ta tell ya 'bout today.

I wish you'd been there fer the healin' part
This evenin'. Both them deacons swear that country
Boy's left leg was gone below the knee,

They saw the nub each time they checked him out
Before the show. I got a rule, ya know,
I never have no truck with, when it comes

Ta healin', folks that's lost a limb. But when
Them deacons tol' me this ol' boy's complaint 'uz
Deefness, wellsir, I can cure that sorta

Ailment in my sleep. Ya get 'em up
In front the crowd with ev'rybody hopin' fer
A miracle, ya get the patient

Primed 'n' eager not ta disappoint the faithful,
Plug his ear-canals with mud,
Then smack him on the ears good 'n' hard,

'N' nine times outa ten, once ya wash
The mud out folks'll claim they're hearin' better, see?
'N' who's ta say they ain't? Not me.

CHARLIE: Yeah, I figured that's the way ya had it rigged.
BUBBA: But this here country boy, Charlie.
              Hell, I saw that bare foot stickin' out

His overalls, a foot that sure 'nough worked, 'cause when
He grabbed my hand 'n' Jesse's too,
'N' started in ta clog, he damn near danced

The boots right off our feet. I asked him after
How much he recalled about the healin'.
Said he recollected when I clapped him

On the ears 'n' he fell flat, but then
He said the rest was like a dream, he felt
His body risin' in the air, right up

Ta heaven, then he heard a voice sayin',
"Hubert Butts, because a your great faith
'N' likewise 'cause the Rev'rend Ray Bob Elray's

Years a faithful service gain great favor in My
Sight, look down there at your trouser leg
'N' find that foot again, the left 'un that got

Pulled inside the thresher, back in August
'83." 'N' then that country boy swore how
He felt that ol' bum leg a his had

Done caught fire it hurt sa bad, but when
He looked, that foot was there a-shinin' like
The sun. That's when the voice said, "Go now,

Hubert Butts, 'n' dance before my tabernacle
Like King David did," 'n' *snap!* the boy
Woke up 'n' there the foot was back. Well, Print,

Ya know how Slim has always said the Lord
Reached down 'n' touched me when I had
That crack-up near Damascus, then reached down

A second time right after Becca
Died when I pert near got lost in sorrow,
Well, ya know, the Lord does things in threes,

'Cause that's His nature, so I've always 'spected
Maybe I'd a third 'un comin'. You don't
Suppose...

CHARLIE: Nawsir, not even fer a minute.

This thing got done. I jest ain't figured how,
But come tomorrow when we brace that country
Boy at that motel, we'll sure 'nough know

Lot more.

BUBBA: But, Print, the Lord a Heaven 'n' Earth
Can do what ere He list.

CHARLIE: Why, Ace, if I
Believed that all it took ta put that fella's

Leg back on was spittin' in his ears 'n' chantin'
"Bully-wooly-willy-wonka-rudy-
Vallee-voulez-vous," I'd say next time

You're on the air, why, you can jes' baptize me there
In front a all your viewers.

BUBBA: Print,
Ya really mean that?

CHARLIE: Jest as sure's my name's

Charles Throckmorton Printwhistle.

BUBBA: Charlie, maybe
That's the Lord's real plan—He let me cure
That cripple, so's the deed 'ud save your soul.

CHARLIE: Why, Ace, that must be it. 'N' here I'se bein'
Dumb 'n' doubtful. Glory gee ta Beezus!

BUBBA: Jes' one problem, Charlie. Don't I recollect

Somebody sayin' years ago how Printwhistle
Weren't your real name after all,
That when ya ran away from home, a-playin'

Bass in wooly chaps 'n' Stetson hat
With that Tex-Mex quartet, Hal Billy 'n' his
Chilibillies, why, ya up 'n' changed it,

Fig'rin' how that switch was easier done
Than your whole fam'ly scramblin' changin' theirs?

CHARLIE: Seems I heard that rumor too. But, Ace,

Ya ain't had nothin' yet ta eat, let's go on down
'N' join the rest, Print needs a big Jack Daniels
He can swim in.

BUBBA: Right behind ya, Throckmorton.

Act Two

(*A radio studio at a country music station in Texas, same as act 1, scene 1.*)

CHARLIE: Hey there! boys 'n' girls, Charlie's back 'n'
Comin' atcha playin' golden oldies.
That last un Charlie spun's a grand ol' number cousin

Floyd Tillman wrote 'n' sung:
"I Love Ya SO-O-O...M-U-C-H...It Hurts Me." Seems
I recollect when I was younger, them bronc

Riders singin', "Gal, I love ya SO-O-O...
M-U-C-H...my back aches!" But that 'uz in another
County. 'Sides, that tough ol' hide's still dead.

Well, folks, enough a Charlie's reminiscin' here,
'Cause lookee yonder who dropped by ta
Say hello. It's Rev'rend Ray Bob Elray—

Plain Big Bubba ta all you fans. You church folks
Recollect how Bubba come ta Waco
'Bout two weeks ago a-preachin' his

Revival—out at Southern Babtist College.
Seems whenever Bubba comes ta town
He always stops ta see his buddy Charlie

Here at W-A-K-O. So, Bubba,

What's the Lord's good work brings ya back this way?

BUBBA: Well, Charlie, all your fine, God-fearin'

Listeners recollect the last time I

'Uz here—'safternoon afore I kicked

My big revival off that night, when lotsa

You good folks come out ta see the Lord's

Weak vessel punch the Devil in the head,

Pin his shoulders ta the mat, 'n' make

That skunk say "uncle" right out loud. But that's

Not all they saw then, Charlie. Guess ya'll heard tell a

How the ev'nin' ended—the hoo-raw

At the healin'.

CHARLIE: Boy-howdy, Bubba, folks

Here 'bouts ain't talked a nothin' since. Fer any

You a-list'nin' don't know yet what Bubba's

Jawin' 'bout, this country boy come up

On stage ta get the preacher's healin' after

Bubba's sermonizin', see. But you

Go on 'n' tell the rest.

BUBBA: Well, folks, this country

Boy 'uz missin' uv a leg, a-hobblin' on a crutch,

But that weren't his affliction, nawsir. Seems

The boy was deef in both his ears...

CHARLIE: So Bubba
He rared back 'n' cast a spell...

BUBBA: Naw, that
Ain't right...

CHARLIE: Scratch that, folks. Then preacher he

Hauled off 'n' jawed a spell.

BUBBA: Hesh up, Charlie!
What I did was call upon the Lord Jehovah's
Name ta heal that pilgrim then 'n' there.

'N' 'cuz the good Lord's power's great
Not only did that deef boy hear again
But later he come bustin' out that room

Back stage where folks passed out from healin'
Get laid up, 'cept now the fella had
His missin' leg back on, a-dancin' like a

Monkey on a skillet, shoutin' "I can
Hear, I can walk."

CHARLIE: But tell what happened then.

BUBBA: Well, 'course, when he danced out on stage,

The whole place just erupted, church folks floppin'
On their knees, the women faintin', shoutin'
Praises...

CHARLIE: Naw, Bubba, that ain't what I meant.

What happened after?

BUBBA: Took a while ta get
The place calmed down, 'n' then I jawed some with
That country boy back stage. Seems the fella

When he fainted had a vision, said the Lord
Done snatched his soul straight up ta heaven, tellin' him
He meant, for reasons of His own,

Ta give him back that foot. Then he woke up 'n'
Sure enough, the foot was there. Well, what
With all the hobblin', healin', faintin', 'n' fancy

Footin', that ol' boy was pert near tuckered out.
The time was gettin' late, so then
I had my people drive this fella straight ta that

Motel outside a town so he could get
Some rest, 'cuz lotsa folks 'ud want ta see
That foot come break a day.

CHARLIE: That's true.

'N' let me tell ya, folks, ol' Charlie'd been
The first in line.

BUBBA: Well, fig'rin' that, I left
A couple deacons there, a-stayin' at that motel,

Ta see this jasper weren't disturbed,
But whatcha know?, some time that night the fella
Used his two good feet 'n' walked away

'N ain't been heard from since.

CHARLIE: Meantime some them folks
At Bubba's show'd been totin' little
Cell phone cam'ras, takin' video pict'res

Right and left, not ta mention live TV.
Why, shoot! the whole shebang went viral on
The internet—Face Tube, You Book, what-not.

When Bubba wakes next mornin' he's
The best known preacher 'cross the land, 'n' that
Ol' country boy's a-bein' hunted high 'n'

Low. So Bubba here he posts a ree-ward:
Anybody knows the whereabouts
A that lost-leggéd-boy-that-was

Jes' turn him in 'n' Bubba'll pay the bounty.
Tell what happened next.

BUBBA: Well, folks, about
Three days ago this *New York Times* reporter

Bubba'd had a run-in with years back
Starts claimin' he's discovered where the fugitive's
A-hidin'—down in some lonesome holler

Back in Eastern Tennessee—but when
He shows up on this yay-hoo's doorstep, whatcha
Know?, he finds not one but two—identical

Twin brothers, 'cept that one'd lost a leg
Below the knee, subtracted in a tractor
Accident when he 'uz just a boy.

Well, when he tells this fella there's a ree-ward
On his head, makin' like the law's
Done posted him, the short leg boy says, ain't

No way that he ner brother Hubert here
Done anything that's wrong, that they 'uz hired
By someone worked at Bubba's TV show.

Boy said his name 'uz Herbert Butts, that he'd
Been paid ta hobble out on stage, a-leanin'
On his crutch pretendin' he 'uz deef,

Then faint when Bubba did the healin'. Said
The fella hired 'em 'ranged ta have his brother
Hubert hide inside that room back stage,

Shut up in a cupboard (almost bent
In two), so hot that poor ol' Hubert pert near
Fainted once or twice afore the deacons

Lugged twin brother Herbert in. Then when
The deacons went ta get a wet towel plus some
Smellin' salts, 'uz when they made the switch.

But Herbert said that ever since his brother'd
Been a boy, he's jes' a dancin' fool,
So, soon as Hubert exited that room,

One shoe on, one shoe off, 'n' heard
The music out on stage, the preacher cloggin'
Like his foot's on fire, the folks out front

A-stompin', clappin', whoopin', shoot!, he couldn't
Hep hisself from jumpin' out on stage
'N' joinin' in. Then Hubert told the *Times*

Reporter how, first step he took beyond
The curtain, Bubba near fell flat, 'n' let me
Tell ya, Charlie, that's the truth. If them

Two deacons hadn't caught me underneath
The arms, I'd a gone down then 'n' there.
So this reporter fella asks, what happened

After? Herbert says that once they'd switched,
Why, he took Hubert's place inside the cupboard,
Hidin' there till folks closed up the hall that night,

When someone come 'n' got him. But what
Chagrined him most 'uz some sneak stole his crutch—
He'd left it in the room, when he climbed in

The cupboard—took it maybe thinkin' it 'uz
Like some holy relic, provin' uv a
Miracle back in them olden days.

At any rate it meant the gent that come ta
Fetch him had ta pert near carry
Herbert far's this fella's car. They drove around

A while till it got late, then went 'n' picked up
Brother out ta that motel.
Fella tol' 'em not ta talk ta no one there,

Then put the two on separate buses back
Ta Tennessee. First thing he knowed folks
Were lookin' fer 'em's when that *Times* reporter

Showed up on their doorstep. Then this here
Reporter asked him who the fella was'd
Hid 'em in the room 'n' took 'em ta

The bus, so Herbert says they never seen
The gent before, but then he says that when
Another, diff'rent fella first approached 'em

Here in Tennessee, a-seein' would
They do this trick, his brother Hubert noticed
Out the window there's another man there

Sittin' in the car, then maybe later's
When ol' Hubert thought this fella looked
A lot like that young pup that Hube 'uz dancin'

With on stage, right upside the preacher.
'Course, this slick reporter jumps on that,
Askin' "Do you mean the preacher's son?"—

Suggestin' maybe Bubba'd somehow set
The whole thing up. But Hubert said he didn't
Think so—reason was, soon's he danced

Down stage 'n' grabbed the fella's hand,
Aimin' ta make him clog with him 'n' Preacher Elray,
Why, he tipped the boy a wink 'n' said,

"Is this the sorta thing ya had in mind?"
That's when the fella looked at Hubert like he's
Sumpin' from the moon 'n' says, "Say what?

Who *are* you, mister?" But that don't satisfy
This slick reporter none, seems this snake's
Got some big axe ta grind, 'swhy he writes

How Hube and Herb'd done been duped once more
By Preacher Elray. That's the reason, folks,
I had ta come back here on Charlie's show

So's I could tell you people what that paper
Said ain't so, that Bubba'd been
The dupe of them two twins, bad Herb 'n' Hubert

	Butts.
CHARLIE:	Ya might say these Butts brothers played

A joke, but cast the preacher as the butt.
Still, these two rubes, sure seems like they 'uz hired

By someone knew his way around back stage.
So tell me, Bubba, whatcha say ta that?

BUBBA: Well, Charlie, Satan never sleeps. 'Bout

A month ago he reared his ugly head
Down there in Houston when them Rice boys slipped
A ringer in amongst them crippled folks

That come up fer the healin'—this young rascal
Made out like he'd fainted dead away,
Then messed his pants with everybody watchin'.

Mark my words, these bumpkin brothers 're both
The devil's tools, 'n' as fer anyone a mine
Participatin', helpin' play

This trick, especi'ly my son Jesse, that's
A lie 'n' that reporter fella knows it.
Why, anybody'd ever seen my show

Or come up fer the healin' knows we keep
A room backstage fer them that's overcome.
'N' 'sides, that hall at Southern Babtist School

Ain't never locked. Why, anyone had a mind ta
Coulda slipped ol' Hubert in
'N' clapped him in that cupboard. Nawsir, folks,

You got my hand ta God—Bubba didn't
Have no part in none a this.
CHARLIE: Well, preacher,
Will ya take some calls? I know our list'ners all 'ud

Like ta jaw a spell with Bubba.
BUBBA: Proud to, Charlie.
CHARLIE: 'Fore we get ta that, why,
Charlie's gonna spin another disc,

Then take a break for sponsors' ads so's we
Can make some money, then the news, then me 'n'
Bubba'll be right back. But you folks know,

Whenever preacher comes ta visit Charlie's
Show, he always asks to hear a song
Mentions the good Lord's name. So here's

The latest hit from Blakey Selden—most requested
Tune by all you vet'rans from Iraq:
"Ain't No Atheists in Foxholes, Lord—

But by God! Ain't No Foxes Neither."
Okay, Ace, we're off the air. So tell me,
Whatcha think? did Nicky have a hand in this?

BUBBA: Hard ta say, seems like this switchin' off two
                 Twins has young Nick's scent all right.
CHARLIE: I know.
                 Slim told me what he'd do when him 'n' Jess

                 'Uz boys.
BUBBA: Nick always was a rascal, Charlie.
                 That's one reason I come by today.
                 Since he left, he's hard ta get in touch with.

CHARLIE: I thought ya threw him out.
BUBBA: Yeah, well, that too.
                 But last time I was on, the boy called in,
                 Pretendin' like he's someone else, so I jes'

                 Figured, Charlie, if I came back on,
                 Why, maybe he'd call in again 'n'
                 Then, if he's pretendin', he'd say somethin'

Tipped his hand, show he's th' orn'ry jasper
Pulled this trick, maybe crow about it.
Then I'd know fer sure.

CHARLIE: Then what?

BUBBA: Why, then

I could disown the boy right on the air.

CHARLIE: That's kinda stiff, ain't it, Ace? Whatcha
Think young Donna'd say ta that?

BUBBA: Well, you

Can ask her, Charlie. Donna drove me here
Today. I left her downstairs in the lobby.
I expect she'd say, if Nicky'd pulled this stunt,

The boy's done set his face against
The Lord 'n' bein' called out on the radio's
The least young Nick deserves, 'speci'lly

If it makes him change his ways.

CHARLIE: So what's
This all about?

BUBBA: Ya know how Nick was always
Needy as a child. Well, Becca used ta

Give him more attention, spoil him some.
But when she died, I had my hands full, travelin'
Preachin' my revivals, raisin' Donna,

Nicky, Jess, I couldn't give the boy
The extra time he wanted, way his momma
Had, that's when he took ta cuttin' up ta make me

Take some notice, always bumpin' up
The ante if I didn't till I had ta
Say enough. I love the boy,

But, Charlie, fer the life a me, I don't
Know how ta handle him.

CHARLIE: Well, I expect
You ain't the first Pa's had that problem, Ace.

But hold on just a minute while I do
The next commercial. Hey there, folks, that Blakey
Selden's sumpin', ain't he? Wrote that tune

Hisself. 'N' all you vet'rans from Afghanistan
Know he ain't a-woofin'—speakin' a which,
Not every soldier been in combat

Comes back home the same, nawsir. 'Swhy
The folks 'round here been grateful through the years—
Since 1925—fer all the caring

Folks down there at Dinkelmeyer's Funeral
Parlor. Now you take that word "parlor," what's it
Call ta mind? You're right—them olden days

When folks laid out their kin in their own home,
The coffin up on trestles in the parlor,
Loved one there inside, jest restin' on a

Bed a ice ta keep from gettin' ripe—
That homey feelin'—can't nothin' take its place.
'N' that's the care ya get from folks down there

At Dinkelmeyer's. No one Charlie's ever
Heard uv found a fault with folks at Dinkelmeyer's
'Bout the treatment uv a loved one. Fam'ly

Biz'ness owned 'n' operated
Pert near ninety years, three successive
Generations—grandpa, son, 'n' grandson,

With a fourth about ta come on board.
Time now fer headline news, so Charlie's
Gotta cut away, but he'll be back with Bubba,

Takin' calls afore ya know it.

BUBBA: Are we off?
CHARLIE: Jes' now. The network does the newsbreak.
BUBBA: Ya know, I knew ol' Grandpa Dinkelmeyer.

Back then the funeral parlor's motto, painted
On the awning right out front,
Was "Just One Loving Fam'ly to Another"—

See, Charlie, that's the thing I had in mind
Once me and Slim got started on the road—
That some day, if the Lord saw fit, there'd be

This fam'ly biz'ness, me 'n' Becca with the boys,
Then Becca's sister, brother-in-law,
Plus young Donna there a-singin' in

The choir, 'n' then this here Pure Products—
Like a legacy left ta keep ol' Bubba's
Ministry afloat once I'd leapt

Ta glory, traded these here brogans fer a pair a
Golden slippers, dancin' with the Lord.
Wellsir, I swear if Nicky's rigged

This stunt ta shame his Pa, makin' like
I had a hand in this here biz'ness with the twins,
Then, Print, he's been a serpent all these years,

Hidin' in the grass, set ta bite.
Fam'ly biz'nes, shoot!, it's like
The prophet says, "Ya wanta hear God laugh,

Jes' make your plans."

CHARLIE: We're comin' back now, Ace.
Hey there! all you country music fans,
Time ta take some calls so folks can jaw

A spell with Bubba, 'member the number here is
254-Ol'-Print. Caller one,
You're on the air.

CALLER ONE: 'Zat you, Charlie?
CHARLIE: Yes, it is,

Darlin', whatcha wanna ask
The preacher?

CALLER ONE: Bubba, can ya hear me?
BUBBA: Yessum,
Loud and clear.

CALLER ONE: Well now, when I came back

From grocery shoppin' twenty minutes ago
The kitchen radio was on 'n' you two
Started tellin' 'bout them bad Butts brothers,

How they'd played a trick on preacher. Well, I
Noticed, 'mongst the veg'tables come tumblin'
Out my shoppin' bag, a big ol' yella squash

'Bout the size a someone's head,
'N' right there pressed upon that yella squash
The blessed face a Jesus jes' a-lookin' at me.

CHARLIE: Oh my!
CALLER ONE: Yessir! Then He began
Ta whisper, said ta call 'n' tell his prophet Bubba
Them Butts brothers was possessed,

That Satan'd sent twin demons straight from hell
Ta try the preacher's faith. He said, ta prove
Them Butts 'uz pixylated, Bubba had ta

Get them two back down ta his revival,
Make 'em come up fer the healin',
So he could cast them demons out.

CHARLIE: Well, sis, what I

Hear tell a drivin' demons outta folks,
Ya got ta know them bad boys' names, seems like
I saw that in a movie once, 'n' Bubba'd better

Wear his raincoat, case those Buttses
Start ta levitate, then upchuck green pea soup
In preacher's face. By any chance

Did Jesus say them demons' names?

CALLER ONE: He did.
He said they's names was Alderbush 'n' Balderdash.

CHARLIE: Whoa! I know them two! Seems like

As soon's I have one drink too many them boys
Show up.

CALLER ONE: Well, shame on you then, Charlie Printwhistle!

CHARLIE: I'm jes' an earthen vessel, sister. The preacher here's

The one whose lips've ne'er touched liquor so ya
Know they could touch yours.

CALLER ONE: Then shame
On you again! Bubba, Charlie's makin'

Sport a me! But you believe me, dontcha?

BUBBA: Sister, I believe the Lord a this here
Universe can do whatever thing

He pleases. Why shucks! If He can shout out through a
Burning bush, then sure 'nough He can
Whisper through a yella squash. Ya see

If He's a mind to, He could set that gourd
A-talkin' clear as Kukla, Ollie, or maybe
Charlie McCarthy—Print here's high-toned cousin.

CHARLIE:　　Yes, 'n' listen, sister, should you run across
Them twin hell demons Burningbush 'n'
Bandersnatch you tell 'em Charlie says

Ta jes' lie low 'cause there's a talkin' squash has
Got their names 'n' Bubba Elray's on
Their trail.

BUBBA:　　　　　　　But, sister, though I do believe

The Lord can speak ta any soul in His creation,
Still I'd say if He decides ta jaw in ways
Most folks 'ud likely call peculiar, well,

The things He says 'ud prob'ly jest apply
To that one soul. He said ta call 'n' tell me
'Bout them demon twins 'n' that's jes' whatcha

Did, so, sis, ya done your duty by
The Lord 'n' Bubba says, "God bless ya!"

CALLER ONE:　　　　　　　　　'N' God bless
You too, Bubba, 'n' God help that Charlie Printwhistle!

CHARLIE:　　Glory gee ta Beezus, sis! 'n' listen, whatever
Ya do, don't cook that squash. Caller Two,
You're on the air.

CALLER TWO:　　　　　　Charlie, I got a question—

I heard you two there talkin' 'bout that trick
Them Buttses played 'n' how that *Times* reporter
Wondered whether Bubba's son, 'n' maybe

Bubba too'd, had a hand in this, tryin' ta
Make like preacher'd really put
That fella's foot back on. Well now, I got ta

Thinkin', there's this story in the Bible—
First Book a Samuel, chapters two to four—
Calls ta mind this case, 'n' 'swhy I wondered

Whether preacher saw this same resemblance?

BUBBA: (*Under his breath to Charlie.*) I think it's him, tryin' ta
hide his voice.
Well now, Caller Two, fer all them folks

Ain't got their Bibles handy, lemme jes'
Remind 'em what ol' Samuel says. He tells
The tale a Eli, priest at Shiloh where they

Keep the Ark, 'n' two a Eli's sons,
One called Hophni, t'other Phinehas, 'n' both a
Them'uz priests like pa, but bad 'uns.

Ya see, what them two boys 'ud do 'uz steal
The meat them Israelites had sacrificed,
Lift it off the altar while the goat was

Still a-smokin', next these rascals, bold
As brass, 'ud fornicate with women hangin' out
Outside the tabernacle door.

Well, when their pa heard tell a these here
Goin's-on, he read them boys the riot act,
But like the Good Book says, "They hearkened not

Unto their daddy's word." That's when the Lord Jehovah
Thought He'd teach 'em both a lesson,
So He killed 'em. Raised a host a Philistines

'N' sent 'em cross the border so's
The Israelites 'ud have ta fight 'em hand ta hand 'n'
Took a turr'ble beatin' that first day.

Right quick, they sent for reinforcements, had
The sons a Eli tote the Ark there
Jest a-huffin' 'n' a-puffin'

Inta camp 'n' when the soldiers saw it,
Why, they shouted out real loud 'n' scared
The Philistines sa bad they pert near messed

Their britches on the spot. But 'cause the Lord
A Hosts had set His face against the sons
A Eli, folks, the Israelites was doomed.

Next day the Jewish side lost thirty thousand
Footmen slain.

CHARLIE: (*Under his breath to Bubba.*)

                    Not ta mention all their
Butlers, plus a truck load full a valets.

BUBBA: (*Under his breath to Charlie.*)

Hesh up, Charlie! What the Lord did, folks,
'Uz jes' permit an awful slaughter so's
Ta kill the sons a Eli. Not only that,

He let the Ark be taken. Meantime back
At Shiloh Eli's sittin' in his high chair
Jest outside the temple gate, waitin'

Ta hear the news, when this here messenger
Comes runnin' up 'n' says the Israelites been
Flattened, both sons 'uz dead, 'n' low 'n' behold

The Phil'steins got the Ark. Well, jest imagine
How ol' Eli felt. He said, "Oh, Lord!,"
Then smacked his forehead with his hand sa hard

He tilted backwards from his high chair, fell
'N' broke his neck. Now, Caller Two, care ta tell me
How this story calls ta mind

That trick the Buttses played or slurs the *Times*
Reporter cast on Bubba's sons' good names.
CALLER TWO: Well, preacher, guess you've heard that sayin' goes,

"The father's truth revealed in the sons' deeds."
Now Eli didn't discipline his boys,
Leastways not so's to make the caution stick.

'N' 'cause he didn't, the Lord a Hosts tipped him
From his seat on high 'n' broke his neck.
'N' that's a warnin', preacher—all them folks

That set themselves high up're fixin' fer a fall.
But more, the reason Eli didn't cast
His sons out, after all their thievin'

Plus their whorin', seems ta me, 'uz 'cause
The old man prob'ly longed ta do the same when
He 'uz young but didn't dare, yet sinned

Within his heart. That's why when it come time
Fer punishin' his boys, he let 'em skate.
But seems ta me I recollect the preacher

Has twin sons, 'n' this last caller claims
The devil sent two demons that possessed
Them bumpkin twins jes' ta test the preacher:

'N' one a them wuz hale 'n' one wuz halt
But preacher couldn't tell the diff'rence, thought they's
Both one man. 'N' seems ta me that says

A lot about another set a twins—
Where he can't tell the diff'rence 'tween the one
That's sound 'n' one that's jest like hollow-sounding brass.

BUBBA: Tell me, Caller Two, did you
                   Call in ta jaw about the tale a Esau
                   Couple weeks ago when I was on?

CALLER TWO: 'N' what if I did?
BUBBA: Well now, seems ta me
                   You're mighty int'rested in sons 'n' fathers.
                   Why's zat, Caller Two?
CALLER TWO: Well, didn't you say

                   Last time that when the Lord reveals Hisself
                   Ta men it's always as a father.
BUBBA: I did.
CALLER TWO: But one that cuts His son loose, even though

                   The boy a-suff'rin', callin' out ta Him
                   Fer help.
BUBBA: He gave the boy his head ta play
                   The hand he'd dealt, let him sacrifice hisself

                   Fer others—'cause He loved His son,
                   Same as I love mine. My boys are jest about
                   The best thing this ol' preacher ever done.

They're twins but each a them is special, each a them's
A sep'rate person, dontcha know?,
'Swhy I let 'em go their own direction,

Never interfere, but let 'em find themselves.
CALLER TWO: That ain't exactly true now, is it,
Preacher? 'Cause I hear tell how you forbid

Your son ta wed a gal he loved, then run him
Off, disowned him even.
BUBBA: The match weren't fittin'.
The girl's the boy's close kin. Not ta mention,

I'm her nearest relative 'n' legal guardian,
She's under my paternal care.
CALLER TWO: 'Sides the fact she's someone preacher's had

His eye on, maybe had some feelin's fer
That ain't sa fatherly, ya see, now
This son's not there, maybe has intentions

Ain't sa fittin', prob'bly's put a move
On her hisself.
BUBBA: What?! Say what?! Why, you
Dirty, little piece a...
CHARLIE: Whoa! Whoa there!, folks,

Preacher's jest about ta speak
In tongues like he does at his revivals,
Shoutin' things like "Willy-nilly-loosy-

Goosy-holy-moly-tuscaloosa," that—
Or words ta that effect—but what say first I
Play another tune's been climbin'

Up the charts? Here's Spunky Johnson pickin' 'n'
Singin', "If I Had It All…Ta Do Over Again…
I'd Do It All Over You." We're off

The air. Are you nuts, Bubba, cussin' like that
On air? Ya wanta get me canceled?

BUBBA: The dirty,

          Little piece a shi…Say what?!

CHARLIE: Ace,

Are you all right? You don't look so good.

BUBBA: I jes' got dizzy there a minute, Print.

That's when them spaniels come a-flyin' through

The air, fillin' up my shoes with grits.
Can't seem ta stop this pain behind my eye.

CHARLIE: Huh?

BUBBA: The Lord's supposed to keep his servants

Safe, protect that precious place between
Their toes from fillin' up with gravel, be a
Brass-bound buckler 'gainst them damned ol' Spaniards.

Where's my Donna? Where's darlin' Donna?

CHARLIE: Bubba,

Jes' you take it easy. Let me get a
Glass a water for ya. (*Flipping on the intercom.*)
  Leroy, there's

A lady downstairs in the lobby name a Donna.
Don't alarm her none. Jest ask her,
Would she come up here right quick? 'N' Leroy,

'Fore ya go, jes' see if there's some asp'rin
Out there, will ya? So now, Bubba, you were
Sayin' sumpin' 'bout this grits 'n' gravy.

Let's jes' talk a while. We'll get ourselves
Calmed down.

LEROY: (*Opening the door and tossing Charlie a small bottle.*)

That's all we got.

CHARLIE: Thank ya, Leroy.
Here ya go, Ace, let's jes' take a few a

These. They'll help that headache. Here's a glass a
Water. Tell me, what's your fav'rite Bible story—
One that always comes to mind?

BUBBA: Can you believe it, Charlie? What that little
Ingrate said? A son broadcastin' charges
Like that on his Pa.

CHARLIE: Well, Ace, ya know,

The boy's been hurt, he wants ta hurt ya back.

BUBBA: Charlie, when 'djou hang that beaded curtain
'Cross the room. It's swayin' back 'n' forth.

CHARLIE: Never you mind about no curtain. Jes' sit
Quiet 'n' give them asp'rins time ta work.
So what's yer fav'rite Bible story?

BUBBA: Second

Samuel, Charlie—tale a David's children:
Them two brothers Absalom 'n' Amnon,
Plus their sister Tamar.

CHARLIE: Seems I recollect

That yarn from Sunday school. That's
The one where Amnon lusts fer Tamar,
Plays a trick, then takes the gal by force.

Which causes brother Ab to seek out David,
Beggin' him ta put his other son ta death.
But pap says no. So then young Absalom

Decides ta act the man, invitin'
Amnon out ta this here barbecue he's
Throwin', plannin' there ta cut his brother's throat

First chance he gets—then does jes' that.
So David exiles Absalom, till years
Go by 'n' David's ol' pal Joab 'minds

The king he's only got one son remainin',
Best ta make things up. So David brings
His boy back home, 'n' dontcha know, this Absalom

Begins ta curry favor with the mob
Till he becomes their fav'rite, raises
Up an army next, 'n' runs his daddy

Out a town. Well, some a David's folks
Stuck by him still. They took up arms, fixin' fer
Ta fight against the boy, but David

Called his captains all together, sayin'
When they went ta battle not ta harm
A hair a that boy's head, seein' he's

The only son the king has left. Well, soon's
They got ta fightin', David's troops begun
Ta win, 'n' whatcha know, young Absalom

He took off on a mule, a-runnin' fer
His life, but when he rode beneath a tree
His long hair got all tangled in the branches

While the mule jes' kept on goin', left him
Hangin' up there, twistin' 'twixt the earth 'n' sky,
Till Joab come a-ridin' up.

Now spite a what King David said, ol' Jo
Had got ta thinkin' seems, "If I'm the one
Convinced the boss ta bring the boy back home,

Then maybe David figures I'm ta blame
Fer all this hoo-raw Absalom's kicked up.
The boy betrayed my friendship, turnin' on

His pa like that, 'n' put the stink eye on ol'
Jo as King Dave's go-to giver a good advice"—
Which flashed through Joab's mind there quick

As a New York minute while young Absalom
Hung swingin' by his hair there from the tree.
That's when this bad boy makes his last mistake:

He smiles at Joab, jest as if he'd been
A naughty child caught stealin' jam from out the pantry,
Come on by a fav'rite uncle.

So ol' Jo thinks, "Fool me once, shame on
You, fool me twice shame on me,"
He hurls his spear right through the boy's white breast

'N' pins him 'gainst the tree, when all Jo's gang
Pitch in, till Absalom a-hangin' there
Mos' like a porky-pine. Right quick they pry him

Loose, throw his body in a ditch,
'N' cover him with stones. Next Joab rides on
Back ta David, sayin' how he tried ta save

The boy, but you know how it is—"the heat
A combat…lots a collateral damage…" So Bubba,
Zat the Bible tale ya had in mind?

BUBBA: That's the one, Charlie. Couldn't've told
It better fer myself.

CHARLIE: Well, Bubba, given
Present circumstances, let's not even

Go there.
BUBBA: What that boy said—you don't believe it,
Do ya, Charlie? I'll admit I was
Wild one back in them early days, but since

That night that I got saved, I've tried ta live
A good life, dontcha know?
CHARLIE: I believe ya, Ace,
A better life than I have. (*Donna enters the booth.*) Whoa!

Say who's this pretty gal come walkin' in?
DONNA: Hey there, Mr. Charlie. Uncle Bubba,
You OK?
BUBBA: Donna darlin', d'ja hear

What Nicky said there on the air?
DONNA: They had
The radio goin' in the lobby. Jes'
Remember, Uncle Bubba, what the doctor

Said 'bout gettin' so upset. Didja
Take your pill this mornin'?
CHARLIE: I think he's feelin'
Better. Ace'd got a little flustered, seems,

With what that second caller said,
Sorta wadn't makin' sense there fer a minute
So I had him take some aspirins.

Seemed ta calm him down.

BUBBA: Yes, Donna, I took
My pill. I swear, sometimes she's treats me like
A child.

DONNA: Well, you're the only uncle this gal's

Got, 'n' 'bout the only daddy she
Remembers. 'Course I care about ya. Maybe
Baby ya a little.

CHARLIE: Listen, Bubba,

Why not pack it in fer now? Go home 'n'
Rest a bit. Donna here'll drive ya,
Maybe have that doctor come 'n' check

Yer pressure.

BUBBA: Charlie, I'm OK. I can
Finish up.

CHARLIE: No need to, Ace, the show 'uz
Almost done. They're doin' the weather now.

BUBBA: Well, Charlie, if I haven't let ya down...
CHARLIE: Not even fer a minute, Ace. I'll say
Good-bye on air.

BUBBA: I do feel tuckered, Charlie.

Maybe we should head on home. What say,
Donna?

CHARLIE: Sure, sounds good.
DONNA: Thank ya, Mr.
Print, you've always been a friend ta Bubba.

CHARLIE: Don't mention it, darlin'. Y'all drive safe.

BUBBA: Good-bye,
Charlie.

CHARLIE: Good-bye. (*Bubba and Donna leave.*) Hey there!
boys 'n' girls,
That's the weather fer the week. The preacher

Had ta leave right quick, but says good-bye
'N' God bless all you folks. Seems he got this
Call—emergency—had ta go 'n'

Cast a demon out a this young fella
Lyin' in the dirt, frothin' at
The mouth, scratchin' hisself behind the ear

With his left foot. That can't be good. Got ta
Be a demon in there somewhere. Bubba's
Gone but Charlie's here a-playin' tunes

Ya love. Here's that new novelty hit—
The Brazos Bar Flies' "Sweet Gal, I'm Stuck on You—
Like Spit on the Sole a Yer Shoe." 'N', folks, I'd swear

Them Bar Flies been a-drinkin' nonstop when they
Cut this side 'cause second time they sing
The title line that word don't sound like "spit."

Act Two

SCENE TWO

*(The living room of Reverend Ray Bob Elray's home in
Waxahachie, Texas, two days after the previous scene.
Charlie Printwhistle enters from stage left to find Slim
Daniels waiting.)*

CHARLIE: I came away, Slim, soon's I heard the news,
Got a pal ta spell me at the station.
How's Bubba holdin' up?

SLIM: Mister Print,

It's like when Becca died. 'Cept worse this time,
Then he had three young'uns left ta keep him
Goin'. Now there's only one—'n' not

The best un neither.

CHARLIE: What happened? Radio said
The state police suspected alcohol,
Thought the other driver came across the line.

What I'd like ta know was what were those two
Doin' out on 66 that time a night,
Raining heavy like it was?

SLIM: Young Donna got a phone call, said Nicky had ta
See her, could she drive ta Grandview
Right that evenin'. Wellsir, Donna said he sounded

Kinda desp'rate, sumpin' 'bout that last time
Bobby come back all confused from takin'
Phone calls on the air—that's when young Donna

Rang the local doc up, had him come see
Bobby, take his pressure, then right quick
They made him go ta bed. Well, Donna drove ta

Grandview, so's I figure they 'uz comin'
Back together when it happened.

CHARLIE: Guess
Ya heard that second caller, Slim. Seems Bubba

Thought it coulda been Nicky playin' tricks,
Disguised his voice startin' out, but finally
Let the real come through the more he talked.

SLIM: Maybe so, maybe not. All's I
Know's the boy I brung up loved young Donna
Like a sister, Mister Print, Nicky'd

Never shame her, linkin' Donna's name
Ta stuff like that right on the air. No wonder
Bobby come home spittin' nails. 'N' if

She thought her Nicky done that, why'd she go
Ta meet him? No suh, Mister Print, no suh.

CHARLIE: Well, I had some doubts myself. But Bubba

Seemed sa sure. What I say mostly facin'
Things like this is "Cui bono?"

SLIM: Howzat?

CHARLIE: It's Latin, Slim, simply means "Whose profit?"

SLIM: Well, Mr. Print, my Bobby's been the Lawd's
             Own prophet ev'ry since he been a man—
             'N' that's da truth.

CHARLIE: Where's Jess? Thought sure he'd

             Be here, what with all the trouble.

SLIM: Oh, he 'uz here,
             I called him soon's the poh-lice called.
             He come right quick. Together we tried calmin'

             Bobby down, 'cuz he be ragin' somethin'
             Fierce, Mr. Print, his heart 'uz breakin'—
             Jes' like ours. But who's there left ta comfort *us*?

             Bobby fin'lly wore hisself out stormin',
             That's when Jess 'n' me ganged up
             'N' made him go ta bed. Jesse drove down town

             Ta make arrangements for the fun'ral, 'spect
             He be back soon.

             (*Bubba enters wearing a bathrobe and slippers.*)

BUBBA: Thought I heard voices
             Down here. Jesse back?

SLIM: No, Bobby. Look

             Who come ta call. Mr. Print drove over
             Soon's he heard the news.

CHARLIE: How ya doin',
             Bubba?

BUBBA: I don't know jes' how I'm doin',

             Why my heart don't jest explode. Years now
             I've told folks how the Lord don't give a body
             More than he can bear, but this here last 'un's

Got me beat. The Lord done pushed His servant
Past the limit.

SLIM: Shame on you! Hush up now!
His grace is great enough. Didn't I

Love them two 'n' hep ya raise 'em? Ain't
My heart weighed down now same as yours? Don't hear me
Jawin' on the Lawd Jehovah none.

BUBBA: Then *you* hush up! My beautiful, darlin' Donna's
Dead, 'n' Nicky Elray caused it. Seems like
Only yesterday that sweet thing weren't

No bigger than a minute, cryin' helpless
'Cause her ma 'n' pa had died. That's when
She saw me sittin' in my chair a-sobbin' over

Becca. Wellsir, she come runnin',
Climbed up in my lap, put her arms
Around my neck 'n' whispered, "Uncle Bubba,

Don't be sad. You've still got me, 'n' I've
Got you. We'll always be together." I remember
Thinkin', Charlie, "That's about

Half right," that I'd die some day first, or she'd
Get married, go on off to start a fam'ly
On her own, but never thought that little

Gal 'ud go before me.

CHARLIE: Ace, I couldn't
Be sorrier. I know how much she meant ta ya,
How much ya meant ta her. But, Bubba,

You lost Nicky too, you lost your boy.
'N' what's all this about young Nicky causin' it?
He wadn't drivin', was he, Slim?

SLIM: Nawsir. Donna was.
BUBBA: But Nick's the one
Got Donna out there, drivin' late at night
In pourin' rain. 'N' why'd she go? She knew

I wouldn't want her to. Why'd she leave
Her Uncle Bubba fer that rascal—after
What he said?
SLIM: Now, Bobby, I done tol' you,

We don't know that—not fer certain. 'Member
Back the time ya threw young Nicky off the show
Ya tol' the crew how they be run off too

If they's ta pal around with Nick,
Well, two er three a his good buddies up
'N' quit account a that, boilin' mad

They wuz, sayin' they'd get even fer him.
Coulda been one a them.
BUBBA: So you're on Nick's side too—
First Donna, now Slim Daniels. Where's Jesse?

He'll be loyal.
CHARLIE: Ace, ya know, Slim could
Be right. That last revival I was at
Your preachin' took the prodigal son fer text,

Claimin' fathers long fer reconciliation.
Well now, young Donna heard that, Ace.
She knew that tale was jest your way a tellin'

Nick across the airwaves, "Come on home
'N' find forgiveness." So what I think is this:
Young Nick called Donna, sayin' how she knew

Her Nick 'ud never say those things that second
Caller did about his Pa 'n' her,
Never try ta shame his Pa with ringers

Like them demon brothers, Herb 'n' Hubert
Butts, called her 'cause he knew you'd never
Take a call from him, feelin' like ya did.

So what I think is Donna drove
Ta Grandview, angel that she was, ta bring
Her Nicky home 'n' make things right between you two.

BUBBA: Ya really think so, Charlie? Think
            She died jes' tryin' ta make peace?

CHARLIE: Well, like
            The gospel says, peacemakers are the Lord's

Own children, 'swhy they're blesséd. That was Donna,
Sure enough.

BUBBA: 'N' think that second caller
            Wadn't Nick, but one a Nick's mean cronies

A-tryin' ta get even?

CHARLIE: Well, like Slim says,
            Coulda been.

BUBBA: But towards the last that second
            Caller's voice 'gan ta sound a lot like Nick's.

CHARLIE: Hell, Ace, if he knew Nick 'n' he
            'Uz any kind a mimic, dontcha think
            He coulda changed his voice so's he'd sound

	Like Nicky, 'specially when he knew the things
	He'd say 'ud get yer goat so bad ya couldn't think straight?
BUBBA:	So ya think, Print, I got tricked?

CHARLIE:	Could be, Bubba. Very well might be.
BUBBA:	So 'cause I lost my temper, cussed my boy,
	Young Donna thought she had ta patch things up

	'N' drove ta Grandview jest ta bring him back,
	So now they're dead together. 'Zat yer point?
CHARLIE:	Well now...
BUBBA:	Lord! Lord! Why dontcha drop

	A mountain on me! Hide me! Leastways, turn
	Yer face away! 'Cause I can't take no more.
SLIM:	Hush up, Bobby! Ya got's ta take whatever

	Trial the Lawd decides. I thought I heard
	Young Jesse's car jes' now. Prob'ly finished
	Makin' 'rangements 'bout the funeral. (*Jesse enters.*) Look

	Who's here, Jesse. Mr. Charlie come ta call.
JESSE:	How are ya, Mr. Print?
CHARLIE:	I came
	As soon's I heard.
JESSE:	I knew ya would, we sure

	Appreciate it. Daddy, how ya feelin'?
BUBBA:	'Bout the same. Dja make arrangements fer
	The fun'ral like we said?
JESSE:	There's somethin' we need

	Ta talk about—out in the other room.
BUBBA:	Naw, Jesse, let's talk here. Slim's fam'ly,
	Charlie's always been a friend. Besides

He jest drove all the way from Waco here.

JESSE: Well, Daddy, seems like when they crashed, the car
Caught fire 'n' they 'uz trapped. That means a closed

Casket fer 'em both. I knew I had ta
Tell ya now, sir, didn't want the sight
Ta shock ya, not in front a all them folks

Who're comin' fer the fun'ral.

BUBBA: What're you sayin',
Jesse?

JESSE: When the first car hit 'em head-on,
One behind 'em couldn't stop in time,

The road was slick some from the rain, the impact
Jest accordioned Donna's car 'n' set
The gas tank off. They couldn't get out.

BUBBA: Say what!?

You mean my baby girl 'n' Nick 'uz burned alive?

JESSE: Yessir.

BUBBA: World, world, O world!
The Lord done cursed me fer my sin! Done made

His servant stand fer an example, can't no
Deed however secret 'scape His sight.
But punish me, Lord. Why punish them? 'N' how come,

Jesse, when the poh-lice phoned, they didn't
Tell us that?

SLIM: They did, Bobby. I took
The call. You come back so worn out from Mr.

Charlie's show that Donna 'n' ol' Doc Gamble
Had ta put ya right ta bed. I figured
News like that 'uz bound ta do ya in,

'Swhy I didn't tell ya, thought maybe if I'd
Wait, there'd be a better time. But Jesse's
Right, better hear it now than at the fun'ral.

BUBBA: Ah, Slim, Slim, our darlin' Donna's
Gone. Jest think how scared she musta been
There at the end, our little girl still conscious,

The car on fire. My God! That picture's gonna
Haunt me till I die, I'll wake 'n' hear her
Screamin' in the flames.

SLIM: I thought a that.

I hope if Donna weren't unconscious, Nick
Who loved her, had the sense to lean across
'N' knock her out before the fire got to her.

BUBBA: Nick' s the brave 'un, he'da done it sure,
If he'd had time ta think. Oh, God! Oh, God!

(*Bubba staggers and seems about to fall when Jesse
catches him under the arms and holds him up.*)

JESSE: Daddy, Mr. Print will understand,

I think we'd better get you back ta bed
'Fore you collapse.

CHARLIE: Sure, Bubba, get some rest,
The fun'ral's gonna use up all your strength.

BUBBA: But, Charlie, see what I mean? About
The curse?

CHARLIE: Well, Bubba, you know me, know Print ain't
Never had no truck with curses. Now,

Coincidence—well, that's another thing.
Some folks might say how you 'n' your whole fam'ly
Ain't been lucky when it comes ta cars.

First, that crack-up in Damascus, then
The wreck that took Rebecca, Donna's parents too,
Fin'lly this here awful crash.

I couldn't feel sorrier, Ace, if Nick 'n' Donna'd
Been my own, but what's the good a talkin'
'Bout a curse? You're tryin' ta make a simple

Accident make sense by fig'rin it's
A punishment fer sin. That don't help no one.
There ain't no hidden reason 'cept some guy

Got drunk 'n' drove, 'n' ran his car across
The road when it was wet 'n' then some other
Man behind 'em couldn't stop. That's all.

BUBBA: Charlie, dontcha know, His eye's on every
            Thing 'n' everyone each second since
            The world began? Not a sparrow falls

            Unless He wills it, no. He's got a plan,
            Lord God has reasons. What they are can't never
            No one know fer sure. Still we can wonder.

            Why, if I believed that this was jest
            Bad luck, that dyin' like that didn't have
            No meanin', wellsir, how'd I know if any

            Thing in life had meanin', Print, or worth.
            Why shoot!, I'd be a heathen jest like you.
CHARLIE: Don't wanta argue with ya, Bubba, I know

You're hurtin' worse'n you can say.

JESSE: Yeah, Daddy,

Slim'll help ya back ta bed.

SLIM: Bobby,

Jest you take aholt a me. We goin'

Ta climb the stairs, then maybe we'll kneel down
'N' pray fer Nick 'n' Donna.

(*Bubba turns away and takes a step with Slim.*)

BUBBA: Slim, know who

I wish was here?

SLIM: Whozat, Bobby?

BUBBA: Charlie Printwhistle.

JESSE: What?! Why, Daddy, Charlie's standin'
Right beside me.

BUBBA: Zat you, Charlie?

CHARLIE: In

The flesh.

BUBBA: Sorry—lately I forget things.

CHARLIE: That's all right, you've had a shock.

BUBBA: Know who

I really wish was here?

CHARLIE: Whozat?

BUBBA: Young Donna.

Beautiful, darlin' girl uv all the world.

CHARLIE: Amen ta that!

BUBBA: Thanks fer comin', Print.

CHARLIE: I'll see ya at the fun'ral, Ace.

(*Bubba and Slim exit.*)

JESSE: We sure

Appreciate your drivin' over, means

A lot at times like this.

CHARLIE: Don't mention it,
Glad ta do it.

JESSE: I'd hoped we'd have a chance
Ta talk, jest by ourselves.

CHARLIE: What's on yer mind?

JESSE: Remember how we talked about you actin'
As the spokesman for Pure Products? 'N' how you
Said you'd think on it? Wellsir, now

The situation's changed. 'Cause look, with Nick
'N' Donna gone 'n' Daddy doin' poorly
Like he is, why shoot! I 'spect the whole shebang'll

Fall on me. I'll need some help.
So what I'm thinkin's, hows about, instead of
Playin' music on the air 'n' playin'

Product spokesman on the side, you come
Ta work fer us—let's say, Vice President
In Charge a Marketing. We could double,

Maybe triple what you're gettin' now.
What say, Mr. Print?

CHARLIE: Is now the time,
Ya think, ta bring this up—Nick 'n' Donna

Not even in the ground, 'n' Bubba near
Collapsed?

JESSE: Maybe not, but there's a schedule
Needs attendin' to. The TV show

Goes live again six weeks from now. We need
Ta start in plannin' who'll take over—that's if
Daddy's not recovered. 'Sides the work a

Marketin' Pure Products. Life goes on
No matter what. Strike while the iron is hot.
Now I know, Mr. Charlie, you might

Hesitate 'bout joinin' up with us
Seein' as how you've been a non-believer.
Daddy says you've been a heathen all your life.

That true? You don't believe in God?

CHARLIE: That ain't jest right—that phrase there "all my life."
I don't believe in God, but I'll stand up

Fer His belief. Ya see, I'd give each child
That ideal startin' out, the dream that there's
A lovin' father hid beyond the stars,

Who made the universe yet still takes care a
Each 'n' every one, makes a moral
Order, gives an afterlife so death don't win,

'N' that's what I'd have ev'ry kid
Start out believin', then I'd see how much a that
Life lets 'em each hold on to. Don't think

Jest 'cause I don't believe in God I ain't
Religious. Lookee here, Jess, some years back
I got converted.

JESSE: What religion?

CHARLIE: Why...uh...

Second Nietzschean Church a Joyful Nihilists.

JESSE: Don't believe I'm real familiar
With that denomination. Snake handlers, are they?

CHARLIE: Naw—though come ta think, we do get lotsa
              Suicides, but it's a right big church,
              Growin' all the time, lotsa folks're

              Members don't even know it yet. 'N' say,
              We got us a Golden Rule like you all do.
              Runs like this: "If someone tries ta kill ya,

              Kill 'em first, 'n' if they don't, why, leave 'em
              The hell alone." Works fer most occasions.
              So, Jesse, guess you'd say that I believe

              In God wholeheartedly—jest not that He exists.
JESSE: Well, Mr. Print, I can work with that.
              So whatcha ya think about that job?

CHARLIE: Don't know. It means a really big disruption, Jess.
              I'll have ta ponder it. But in the meantime
              Answer me two questions so's I

              Know jest who I'm dealin' with. Tell me
              What ya know about that second caller
              On the air, the one that knocked ol' Bubba

              Fer a loop. 'N' while you're at it, tell me
              How the fella rigged that trick with them
              Butts brothers knew ta find a set a twins

              With three good legs between 'em. Why shoot!, ya know,
                  Jess,
              When that video went viral after
              Bubba posted his ree-ward, all the

              Newsmen here 'n' yonder set out lookin'
              Fer them two but couldn't find 'em, took
              That fella from the *Times* near three whole weeks

Ta track 'em down in that ol' lonesome holler
Back in eastern Tennessee—'n' even then, why,
Someone had ta tip him off where they 'uz hidin'.

'N' *who* was that? Musta been
The fella that arranged it all ta start.
So whatcha know 'bout that?

JESSE: I don't believe

I get jest what you mean?

CHARLIE: Oh, Jess, I think
Ya do.

(*At this point Slim reenters from stage right.*)

SLIM: Jess, yer Daddy wants ta see ya.
JESSE: Got ta go, Mr. Print, but thanks

Again for comin'. Let me know as soon's
Ya can about that job. (*Jesse exits.*)

SLIM: I heard the last
A what ya said. Reminded me a sumpin' now

I'd clean forgot. When Nick 'n' Jess
'Uz boys, their Ma enrolled 'em in this big
Society a twins, sent 'em off

Ta meetins, summer camp chock-full a look-alikes
Like them. Well, Nicky hated it,
So you jest know Jess couldn't get enough.

When Becca died 'n' Nicky stopped attendin'
Summer camp, then Jesse went without him,
Kept in touch with all them other pairs fer years.

Can't rightly say what made me think a
That jest now.

CHARLIE: So you've begun ta think like me?

SLIM: Got my hands full thinkin' my own thoughts,

Can't think nobody else's.

CHARLIE: Answered
Like a diplomat.

SLIM: Ain't got no diploma
Mr. Print.

CHARLIE: A wise man nonetheless.

(*Charlie exits.*)

Act Two

(*Same setting as previous scene but one month later.*
Slim is in the living room when Charlie enters.)

CHARLIE: Am I the first 'un, Slim?
SLIM: Nawsir, Mr. Print.
Jesse's here. He's in the other room
Talkin' on the phone I 'spect.

CHARLIE: When's the lawyer s'posed ta get here?
SLIM: Any
Time now.
CHARLIE: Took me by surprise when he
Called—said Ace'd put me in his will.

Still can't believe he's gone. Thought sure when he
Collapsed at Nick 'n' Donna's fun'ral, ol' Doc
Gamble said it's jest a minor stroke,

Reckoned he'd recover quick without
No ill effects. That's why when I dropped by
Few weeks ago he seemed like his old self—

Jes' sadder's all.
SLIM: Whatever you two talked about,
My Bobby called the lawyer that next day
So Mr. Rivers drove on out,

Spent that afternoon there jawin' back
In Bobby's study. What did you 'n' Bobby
Have ta say?

CHARLIE: Oh, nothin' much, ya know—

How's he feelin', when's he plan ta start
The ministry again. Told him 'bout
The job young Jess'd offered, mentioned how

I'd had these questions that I'd asked him so's I'd
Know jest where I stood—same concerns
You 'n' me had last time we both talked.

SLIM: I 'spect that's why, soon's you left that day,
My Bobby started aksin' me about
Some things.

CHARLIE: Whadja say?

SLIM: I alwayst tell

My Bobby what I'm thinkin'.

CHARLIE: Betcha do, 'n' then some.
'N' after that Bubba passed?

SLIM: End a that same week there in his sleep.

CHARLIE: Still can't believe he's gone.

(*Enter Jesse from stage right, extending his hand
to Charlie.*)

JESSE: Mr. Print,
The lawyer said you'd be here, seems that Daddy
Aimed ta thank you in his will for all

Your years a friendship, spreadin' word a Daddy's
Preachin'. Uncle Slim, how 'bout fixin' up
A pot a coffee if ya would, sir,

So's we'll be right sociable when Mr.
Rivers comes.

SLIM: Uh-hunh. Well, Mr. Print,
Seems Jesse wants ta talk ta ya alone,

So I'll be in the kitchen, rattlin' pots
Till the lawyer gets here. (*Slim exits.*)

JESSE: Never could
Fool Uncle Slim. So, Mr. Print, last time

We talked you had some questions, seemed ta think
I might know somethin' 'bout them two Butts brothers,
Maybe thought I recognized that caller

On the air got Daddy so riled up.
Now then, I'm not sayin' I do, but just
Suppose that there's a fella has a brother

Looks just like him, Mr. Print, but ev'ry
Other way the brother's diff'rent. Fella
Says yes, brother says no, fella says white,

T'other says black—it's like the only thing
The brother's born for's just ta block this fella
Off at ev'ry turn. So whatcha think

The fella feels 'bout that?

CHARLIE: Why, I'd say over
Time this boy 'ud get plumb peevish.

JESSE: Absolutely!
'N' not just that, this fella's momma always

Liked the brother more. He had a way
A makin' mischief, mostly made his momma
Laugh 'n' then forgive him. 'Course his Pa

Preferred the fella, thought the brother was
A wastrel. Still, that didn't near make up
For all his Momma's pamp'rin' this bad brother

'Stead of him, couldn't, 'cause his Pa
Was on the road so much away from home.
'N' then, to make things worse, Print, while the fella's

Still a boy, his Momma ups 'n' dies
'N' so he never gets to show her when he's
Grown why he's the one she should've trusted,

He's the one she could depend on, steady,
Serious. Wellsir, what come next, his brother
Tries to drive a wedge between their Pa 'n'

Him, seems to think this job's his only
Goal in life, until the fella's pert near
Crazy fig'rin' where the next mean trick

Lies waitin', can't sleep nights expectin' mischief
Any minute. Well, Mr. Print, I ask you,
What's a fella in a fix like that

Supposed to do?

CHARLIE: Well, Jess, I guess the boy's
Jest got ta grin 'n' bear it, else he'd go
Plumb nuts 'n' pull a stunt that folks call drastic.

JESSE: Rightchu are! He holds his piece 'n' helps
His Pa, becomes his Daddy's right-hand man,
Goin' 'bout his Daddy's business ev'ry day,

Waitin' can he see the brother
Tip his hand. 'N' then the brother does—
Somethin' bad enough his Daddy casts him

Out, then casts him off. Meantime the fella's
Busy buildin' up the fam'ly business,
Gets an idea how to spread the word clear

'Round the world about his Daddy's work.
A miracle maybe. Those that don't believe'll
Never give it credence, no. But those

Who do, why, they'll believe no matter what.
So now the fella puts his plan in motion, see,
But wouldnt'cha know? his Daddy starts

To havin' second thoughts about the brother,
Starts to wonder whether he'd been rash
To turn him out that way, that maybe he

Should bring the rascal back, "the prodigal son."
Well now, here's where the fella's plan reveals
Its genius: your true believer'll believe

No matter what, just 'cause he mostly needs to,
While all your skeptics never will, not even
If their hair caught fire from tongues of flame,

So whether his plan works or fails, the fella's
Golden. Matter of fact, the thing works better
If it fails. The faithful'll believe

Even if the thing's absurd. Or, better yet,
Just because the thing's absurd,
Like some ol' churchman said. But all the skeptics,

Once they get a scent the thing's a hoax,
Boy howdy!, they'll broadcast the news forever,
Where before they'd just ignored it. What

The fella sees right then's he's got to help
The thing along, makin' sure it blows
A gasket, so he tips a wink 'n' bang!

The papers get the story, Daddy's plumb
Embarrassed, wond'rin' who's just mean enough
To play a trick like this, 'n' then this fella,

Thinkin' out loud maybe, murmurs, "Could it
Be that ornery brother, wantin' payback
On his Daddy all because he cast him out?"

'N' Daddy says, "Why, sure!" So then
This fella, just to guard against his Pa's
Backslidin', havin' second thoughts again,

Decides he'll put some icin' on the cake.
Ever since he was a boy, his brother'd
Done him dirt, imitatin' how

He talked 'n' dressed, just so's he'd get the boy
In trouble. Listen, two can play that game,
'N' if the brother's voice could sound like his,

Then turnabout's fair play. So let's be clear:
I'm not a-sayin' these things happened, no sir.
I was just supposin' what a person

Naturally suspicious like yourself
Could easily imagine. So, we're good?
CHARLIE: I must say, Jesse, you're a fella after

My own heart. That's why when you're around
I keep my kevlar vest on, buttoned tight.
But here's another question fer that fella

Jest supposin'. Don't he think the plan
He set a-goin' maybe ended up
In somethin' awful, cost two lives, 'n' then

Another after.

JESSE: Maybe so. The fella's
Been debatin' with himself, "Was *he*
To blame?" He didn't cause the rain or drunken

Driver, two-lane highway, midnight hour.
No sir, nothin' tells him he's at fault.
Seems like in such debates, the self most always

Wins. 'Sides the fact the fella has
Big plans to spread his Daddy's business 'cross
The world, with all the good it does—somethin'

The brother never understood 'n' tried
To stop.

CHARLIE: But what about the girl?
JESSE: Wellsir,
That made the fella sad, because she threw in

With the brother. But when you got big plans,
How's the sayin' go? "You wanta make omelettes,
You gotta break legs." It's what they call the law

Of unintended consequences, Print.

CHARLIE: I see. In war I think it's called "collat'ral damage."
JESSE: So now, we understand each other?

CHARLIE: Yeah, Jess, I think we do.

              (*The front doorbell rings.*)

JESSE: There's the lawyer.
              Excuse me just a minute, Mr. Print.

              (*Jesse exits, then Slim enters with a pot of coffee and three
              cups on a tray.*)

SLIM: So you 'n' Jesse have your talk?
CHARLIE: Yessir.

SLIM: Whatcha think?
CHARLIE: Jest what we suspected.
SLIM: I knew it, Mr. Print. Couldn't be
              Nobody else.
              (*Jesse reenters with the lawyer.*)
JESSE: Mr. Rivers, you know

              Charlie Printwhistle.
RIVERS: We've talked some on the phone,
              But never met. Mighty pleased ta meet ya,
              Mr. Printwhistle. (*They shake hands.*) Heard ya on the air

              Fer years, 'n' now we fin'lly get ta meet.
CHARLIE: The pleasure's mine.
JESSE: 'N' a 'course, you do
              Remember Slim.
RIVERS: Oh yeah, Slim 'n' I

              Go back a ways. How ya doin', Slim?
SLIM: Gettin' older by the minute.
RIVERS: Aren't
              We all.
SLIM: Well, now, the coffee's on the table there,

So help yourselves. I'll be in the kitchen
If ya need me.

RIVERS: Naw, Slim, stay here.
'Cause this concerns you too. Didja fix

The VCR?

SLIM: Yessir, Mr. Rivers,
Got it all set up right there.

RIVERS: .   Well, now,
Y'all know why we're here. Bubba's will

Remembers evr'ry one a you—plus Bubba
Taped a message sayin' his good-byes
'N' tellin' what he meant by what he left each one,

So if you all'll have a seat.

JESSE: Yeah, come on in, sit down. Who wants coffee?
RIVERS: None fer me, thanks, Jess.
CHARLIE: Yeah, I'll have some.

JESSE: What about you, Uncle Slim?
SLIM: I had
A cup in the kitchen, Jesse, so I'll pass.
RIVERS: Well, folks, here's what Bubba wanted me

Ta do: first, play the tape, then hand out copies
Of the will, then answer any questions
You might have. So here we go.

(*Rivers put the tape in the VCR and Bubba's face appears
on the TV screen.*)

BUBBA: Y'all know me 'n' know I got ta have
The final word. 'N' if you're seein' this,
I know I'm gone, so we can't have a partin'

Word in person with a handshake or a
Hug. So, Jesse, you're my son that I
Love dearly, always been my fav'rite, carin'

'Bout the ministry, doin' the Lord's
Own work, 'n' maybe sometimes carried away
With zeal, doin' things that weren't quite right.

So, Jess, I think I know jest what ya did
'N' know the human failin' made ya do it.
All I want ta say's your Pa forgives ya—

Can't do no other thing if I've arrived
To where I aimed at all these years—same's
I know jest what *I* did, 'n' ask the Father

Fer forgiveness. Now, Slim, you've known me ever
Since I was a boy, been like a brother
All these years, couldn't ask no better friend.

I want that you should care fer Jess jest like
He's your son, 'n', Jesse, you look after
Slim, same as you would me. Now, Charlie,

I jest bet you're sittin' there, one eyebrow
Raised, your lip a-curlin' right up at the corner
Thinkin' "How did I get here?"

With all these redneck Bible-thumpers. Sure 'nough,
Fer years there on the air, jest pretendin' like
You're down-home folks, ya told yourself

The whole thing was a role, a-smilin' on
The inside, thinkin' how ya had your listeners—
Poor ol' cow-belles, dumb cow-billies—fooled,

Makin' fun a them so's only you
Could know, but thinkin' all the while you're diff'rent—
More sophisticated maybe, man a the world.

But all that time you stayed my friend,
Always had me on your show, always
Plugged my preachin' soon's I came ta town.

I know you figured I was actin' out
A role like you, prob'ly thought professional
Courtesy, one trooper to another,

Print, demanded some reciprocal
Acknowledgment a talent—sort a thing
Those little envelopes I left ya showed.
But what I always liked about ya, Print's,

The way you took my role—a-playin' the Lord's
True prophet—with a great big grain a salt,
Always told me what ya thought no matter what,

Never guessin' all those years
I played the part in earnest. Lotsa times
I told ya how I'd make a Christian uv ya yet.

Well, now's the last chance I'm gonna get
Ta turn that grain a salt there, Print, to one
Whole tablespoon a sugar. So here goes:

I leave ta Jess, my son, the sum a one
Million dollars free 'n' clear. Next,
I leave ta Henry Daniels, the oldest friend I've got,

The sum a half a million dollars,
The fam'ly home in Waxahachie, plus
A pension fer his lifetime. Next, Big Bubba's

Ministry, the syndicated TV
Show, my company Pure Products of
America, Incorporated—I direct

My total int'rest in these entities
Be split as follows: forty-five
Percent ta Jesse Elray, forty-five

Percent ta Henry Daniels, ten percent
Ta Charles Throckmorton Printwhistle. Further I
Appoint this latter individual the sole

Executor a my estate.
His fee, if he agrees ta partner with my son
'N' Slim, 'll be a quarter million

Dollars. If he doesn't, then my lawyer
William Rivers'll fulfill this role,
Receive the fee, plus the ten percent

Partnership share. Now here's what I
Intend: that Jesse, Slim, 'n' Charlie all
Be partners, jest so nothin' major gets

Decided 'lessin' two a you agree.
But what I want's the three a you to work
Together: Jesse has the energy 'n'

Brains, 'n' Slim has always been the heart 'n'
Soul, the kindest 'n' the carin' part,
While Print's the shrewd one, wise 'n' wily, always

Balancin' intent against the means.
So now I'll say good-bye. I'm sorry I had
Ta leave ya, but I trust I'm in a better

Place 'n' hope some day I'll see you all
Again—includin' even you, Charlie Printwhistle.

(*The tape ends and Mr. Rivers turns off the VCR.*)

RIVERS: Well, that's what Bubba had ta say,

'N' here's a copy of the will you each
Can have. So, folks, I'll answer any questions
Now, or if you'd like some time to look it

Over, you can email or jes' call me
At the office. I wonder, Mr. Printwhistle,
If it's too soon to ask 'bout what you're thinkin'—

Bein' sole executor?
CHARLIE: Kinda
Takes your breath away, don't it?
JESSE: Sure 'nough
Knocked the wind right out a me.
CHARLIE: Well now, listen,

Bubba wanted me ta do it,
So I will. Wouldn't be much uv a friend
Ta turn him down once he'd crossed the bar.

So, Mr. Rivers, guess you'll brief me 'bout
The duties uv executors.
RIVERS: Yessir,
Here's my card. 'N', Jess, here's one for you,
'N', Slim, there's one for you. So when you've had

A chance to read the will, if you've got questions,
Ya'll know how to reach me.
CHARLIE: Jesse, looks like
'Stead a workin' for ya, you 'n' me're

Partners.

JESSE: Jes' not equal partners.

RIVERS: Well now,

Unless there's something more we need to talk about,

I'll say good-bye. Mr. Printwhistle,

What's your afternoon look like tomorrow?

Could we meet?

CHARLIE: How 'bout four o'clock?

RIVERS: Sounds good. Address's on the card right there.

So long.

JESSE: Mr. Rivers, I'll see ya to your car.

(*Jesse and Rivers leave together, stage left.*)

SLIM: Whatcha figure that's about?

CHARLIE: Oh, jest Jesse gettin' in some fast

Footwork 'tween here 'n' Rivers' car. The boy

Don't like the split, er me as sole executor,

So he'll be jawin' lawyer Rivers now,

Seein' can he find a way

Ta overturn the will, like maybe Ace 'uz

Still so groggy losin' Nick 'n' Donna,

Seems he didn't know what he 'uz doin'

Leavin' Jess, his one remainin' son 'n'

Heir, so little uv the family business.

That's the sorta story he'll be tellin'

Rivers now, remindin' him about

The fee if Rivers's got ta take the job on.

Think he'll have much luck?

SLIM: Jesse, don't
Know Mr. Rivers if he thinks that sorta
Thing'll work.

CHARLIE: Yeah, Slim, that's my impression

Uv the man. But still in all, ya never
Know fer sure what folks'll do when money's
On the table. Looks like you 'n' me're

Meant fer partners. Don't suppose I'll haveta
Be ordained ta count collection baskets.
Never been a minister before,

Maybe it'll make my character
Improve, ya think?

SLIM: Nawsir, you's still a heathen,
Jest like Bobby said.

CHARLIE: Why, hell yes, Slim,

Jest not a disint'rested heathen any more.
Besides I think I know what Bubba had in
Mind, cuttin' me a slice. He figured,

Knowin' Jesse, if the two a you 'uz
Partners by yourselves, his old pal Slim
Might jest end up collat'ral damage or else

An unintended consequence, so Bubba
Threw me in the mix, fixin' things
So you 'n' me could slow up Jesse if

He tried ta pull a fast one. 'N' then who knows?
We might even do some good.

SLIM: Ya think so,
Mr. Print?

CHARLIE: Not impossible, but not

Much likely. I'll be happy jest ta keep
Us both from goin' ta the pen in one
A Jesse's schemes. But look here, Slim, that means

You got ta watch my back, 'cause I'll watch yours.
'N' that's what Bubba wanted.

SLIM: Well, Mr. Print,
That way ain't nobody sneakin' up on either.

CHARLIE: But answer me one question, Slim.
Bubba said jest now he thought he knew
What Jess had done 'n' still forgave him, then went on

Ta say how he knew what *he* had done
'N' prayed the Father'ud forgive him too,
He didn't mean that thing the second caller

Said about him lustin' after Donna,
Did he? 'Cause I'd really like ta know.
I'd hate ta think the man I called a friend

Fer all these years 'uz like that, hate ta have
That stain his mem'ry when he comes ta mind.

SLIM: Well, Mr. Print, since you was Bobby's friend

'N' you 'n' me is partners now 'n' all
The folks this tale could hurt're dead 'n' gone,
I guess there's no harm tellin'. Bobby

	Always had this special thing fer Donna.
CHARLIE:	I know—his only niece, adopted daughter both,
	Once her parents died.
SLIM:	Nawsir,

	Bobby's niece 'n' natural daughter too.
CHARLIE:	What?
SLIM:	Yessir, Bobby was her father. Happened
	Twenty-five years ago. Becca 'n'

Bobby had some trouble 'roun' that time,
So Becca asked her parents could she come back
Home a spell, 'n' took the boys back with her.

Bobby felt real bad, missed her sumpin'
Dreadful. Becca's sister Bonnie tried ta
Comfort Bobby, maybe tried too hard.

Bonnie wanted children. She 'n' Bill,
The husban', tried fer years. Nothin' ever
Happened, so I guess she figured Bill 'uz

Shootin' blanks, why not try a diff'rent
Pistol, Mr. Print. But keep it in the fam'ly.
That's where Bobby come ta mind.

He was lonesome, she was willin', didn't
Last fer very long. Becca come back
Six months later with the boys, she

'N' Bobby made things up, young Donna come
Along 'bout three months after that.

CHARLIE:	How many
	People knew 'bout this?
SLIM:	Only Bobby,

Bonnie, 'n' me.

CHARLIE: How'd you find out?

SLIM: Bobby
Pert near lost his mind when Becca 'n' Bonnie
Died, plus Bonnie's husban' (that 'uz drivin'),

Stayed awake two nights, talkin', cryin',
Sayin' how the Lawd done punished him
By takin' both the sisters off, but left

The fruit a his adultery behint
Jest so's he'd not forget his sin 'n' shame.
That's why he had this special love fer Donna,

Never tol' her he's her natural Pa
But cared fer her lots more than both the boys,
'N' 'swhy, when she 'n' Nick 'uz killed, my Bobby

Figured how the Lawd done punished him
The third 'n' final time—first that crack-up
Near Damascus when He raised him fer a prophet,

Then the wreck that took the sisters
'Cause a Bobby's fleshly failin', last
This crash that killed his children 'cause he never

Tol' the truth about the way his Nick
'N' Donna 'uz related. Ya see now why,
When Nicky started sayin' how he meant

Ta marry Donna, Bobby plumb forbid it,
Fin'lly had ta run young Nicky off.
The only reason Bobby didn't lose

His mind when Nick 'n' Donna died 'uz 'cause
He thought the Lawd done punished him enough
Down here ta wash away his sins, so when

He met 'em all again—the ones he loved
'N' wronged—they'd understan', forgive him maybe.

CHARLIE: So that's what Bubba meant, admittin' how

He knew the thing he'd done 'n' askin' fer
Forgiveness.

SLIM: That's it, Mr. Print.

CHARLIE: You don't
Suppose young Jess got wind a this?

SLIM: I don't

See how he coulda. Still he knew how Bobby
Felt about first cousins gettin' hitched,
'N' knew how Bobby idolized young Donna,

Maybe figured what that second caller
Said'ud get ta Bobby bad. Still can't
Believe that Jesse'd have a hand in that.

CHARLIE: Well, I don't know, Slim, seemed ta me that Jess
As good as said so.

SLIM: If he did, I'll never
Trust that boy again.

CHARLIE: Best not.

(*Jesse reenters, stage left.*)

JESSE: Well, Mr.

Rivers jes' 'bout talked my ear off.

CHARLIE: 'Swhat
I figured. Fella struck me as a real ol'
Chatterbox.

JESSE: Now since we've Daddy's blessin'

From the grave, I say let's us proceed
With faith unshaken, partners, savin' souls.

CHARLIE: You betcha, Jesse, even if Slim here

Might think those words resemble ones were used
By some sly wit about them ol' unshakables
Fox-huntin' what's incredible.

SLIM: Never thought no

Such thing.

CHARLIE: Well, pards, what say we rustle up
Some souls, hog-tie, 'n brand'em? Let's have a holy
Rodeo! Wah-hoo, Jesse! Yee-hah, Jesus!

About the Author

John Bricuth is the pen name of John T. Irwin, the Decker Professor in the Humanities and former chair of the Writing Seminars at Johns Hopkins University. He is the author of numerous works of literary criticism and poetry, including *Just Let Me Say This About That, As Long As It's Big, Hart Crane's Poetry: "Appollinaire lived in Paris, I live in Cleveland, Ohio,"* and *F. Scott Fitzgerald's Fiction: "An Almost Theatrical Innocence."* The editor of *The Hopkins Review*, he is a member of the American Academy of Arts and Sciences.

Poetry Titles in the Series

John Hollander, *Blue Wine and Other Poems*

Robert Pack, *Waking to My Name: New and Selected Poems*

Philip Dacey, *The Boy under the Bed*

Wyatt Prunty, *The Times Between*

Barry Spacks, *Spacks Street, New and Selected Poems*

Gibbons Ruark, *Keeping Company*

David St. John, *Hush*

Wyatt Prunty, *What Women Know, What Men Believe*

Adrien Stoutenberg, *Land of Superior Mirages: New and Selected Poems*

John Hollander, *In Time and Place*

Charles Martin, *Steal the Bacon*

John Bricuth, *The Heisenberg Variations*

Tom Disch, *Yes, Let's: New and Selected Poems*

Wyatt Prunty, *Balance as Belief*

Tom Disch, *Dark Verses and Light*

Thomas Carper, *Fiddle Lane*

Emily Grosholz, *Eden*

X. J. Kennedy, *Dark Horses: New Poems*

Wyatt Prunty, *The Run of the House*

Robert Phillips, *Breakdown Lane*

Vicki Hearne, *The Parts of Light*

Timothy Steele, *The Color Wheel*

Josephine Jacobsen, *In the Crevice of Time: New and Collected Poems*

Thomas Carper, *From Nature*

John Burt, *Work without Hope: Poetry by John Burt*

Charles Martin, *What the Darkness Proposes: Poems*

Wyatt Prunty, *Since the Noon Mail Stopped*

William Jay Smith, *The World below the Window: Poems 1937-1997*

Wyatt Prunty, *Unarmed and Dangerous: New and Selected Poems*

Robert Phillips, *Spinach Days*

X. J. Kennedy, *The Lords of Misrule: Poems 1992-2001*

John T. Irwin, ed., *Words Brushed by Music: Twenty-Five Years of the Johns Hopkins Poetry Series*

John Bricuth, *As Long As It's Big: A Narrative Poem*

Robert Phillips, *Circumstances Beyond Our Control: Poems*

Daniel Anderson, *Drunk in Sunlight*

X. J. Kennedy, *In a Prominent Bar in Secaucus: New and Selected Poems, 1955-2007*

William Jay Smith, *Words by the Water*

Wyatt Prunty, *The Lover's Guide to Trapping*

Charles Martin, *Signs & Wonders*

Peter Filkins, *The View We're Granted*

Brian Swann, *In Late Light*

Daniel Anderson, *The Night Guard at the Wilberforce Hotel*

Wyatt Prunty, *Couldn't Prove, Had to Promise*